Celebrating the Land

Celebrating the Land

Women's Nature Writings, 1850–1991

Edited by Karen Knowles

NORTHLAND PUBLISHING

For Brian
And in memory of Betti Albrecht

FIRST EDITION
Second Printing, 1993
ISBN: 0-87358-545-3
Library of Congress Catalog Card Number 92-13071

Cover illustration © 1992 by Mary Beath
Cover design by David Jenney
Text design by Carolyn Gibbs

Library of Congress Cataloging-in-Publication Data
Celebrating the land : women's nature writings, 1850-1991 / edited by
Karen Knowles. -- 1st ed.
144 p.
Includes bibliographical references (p.131–133).
ISBN 0-87358-545-3 (pbk.) : $12.95
1. Natural history. 2. Nature stories. 3. Women authors. I. Knowles, Karen.
II. Title: Women's nature writings.
QH81.C38   1992
508'.082--dc20   92-13071

Manufactured and Printed in the United States of America

6-93/5M/0453

Contents

Contents

*author's birth date unavailable

ACKNOWLEDGMENTS

I WISH TO THANK DEPAUL UNIVERSITY for my research grant; Linda Furbush for typing the manuscript; Daniel Furbush for his technical assistance; my colleagues Linda Hillman, Eileen Seifert, Nancy Freehafer, and Mary Miritello for their consistent support; and Jessie Grearson Sapat for her enthusiasm and careful reading of the manuscript. I am grateful, also, to Brian Knowles for his insightful comments on the manuscript in its several stages, and for sharing with me his love of the natural world.

INTRODUCTION

I HAVE YET TO KEEP BEES on a southern Missouri farm or herd sheep on a Wyoming ridge. Even so, I can imagine how it feels to stand near an apple tree on a spring day and be enveloped by a swarm of bees; or to spend three days alone herding two thousand sheep for the first time, my skin burned from the sun, my attention focused because I must learn to read the landscape and move those sheep to a grazing range.

These experiences become so real because Sue Hubbell and Gretel Ehrlich invite us to share their personal encounters with the land. Their vivid descriptions of the natural world have heightened my own appreciation of nature. In fact, it was Sue Hubbell's *A Country Year: Living the Questions* (1986) that first inspired me to read other nature writing by women.

Around the same time as I was reading *A Country Year*, I heard Gretel Ehrlich read from her work-in-progress during a conference in a Chicago hotel. Her lyrical writing transported me from the conference room right into a Wyoming winter. All I had to do was close my eyes to shut out the room's chandeliers and naugahyde chairs and I could see the beauty she knows so well, feel the memories the land holds for her. It was difficult to return to that Chicago hotel.

Both Hubbell's and Ehrlich's writing, so rich in personal and natural history, captured my imagination and sent me in search of women's experiences in the American landscape.

I find the twenty writers collected here engaging in three significant ways: each writer tells of her personal quest to live in harmony with the land; each writer captures a moment through wonderfully descriptive detail; and each writer shares her memories of the land. Some describe experiences I envy: camping in the Utah desert; taking a river trip in the Florida wilderness; living on the shores of a mighty Alaskan river. Some describe experiences I've shared: waiting impatiently for springtime in New Hampshire; watching great thunder clouds race across the Minnesotan sky; tasting sap from sugar maple trees during a spring thaw. But all of these writers provide important insights into the diversity of the natural world.

Women have long been stereotyped as "indoor creatures"—at home only in the home. I have selected women's writings from 1850 through 1991 that suggest the opposite is true: Women have long explored the natural world and written about their experiences within it. From the essays collected here, a new picture of women from the past two centuries emerges; these are women who enjoy both the beauty and danger inherent in the natural world, and their stories challenge the cultural perception that women are uninterested in science or natural history.

As I researched women's nature writing, I was astonished to discover the volume of work available from the past two centuries. Although most general nature anthologies reprint the same few women's work repeatedly, and tend to include that of more recent writers, there is an abundance of nature writing by women. They may be scientists, farmers, gardeners, or naturalists, but their work shows women involved in the "outdoor" world. From this diverse collection of material, I have chosen popular nature writing over the past two centuries that emphasizes women's sense of place in the American landscape. The chronological arrangement of this anthology reflects natural history—the land as it has existed over the past two centuries—and women's history—the ways in which women travelled from the East to western, frontier lands, including Alaska.

These women's essays, letters, and journals invite us to visit a cherished place. Through them we immediately have a feel for the landscape—we learn its stories, we see its beauty, and we share with each writer her connection to the land. Each writer focuses on a particular geographical location in America, but the collection shows a diversity of natural settings: the mountains of Colorado, the deserts of the Southwest, a marsh in Maryland, a river in Florida or Alaska, or a farm in New England or Missouri. Some writers are most interested in animals as part of the landscape, others in the plants and flowers of forest and field.

But all share one important definition of landscape: they consider themselves part of the natural world rather than distant and emotionally detached from it. Leslie Marmon Silko characterizes this best in her essay "Landscape, History, and the Pueblo Imagination" (1984), in which she explains the ancient Pueblo Indian belief that "The land, the sky, and all that is within them—the landscape—includes human beings." This interrelationship is depicted in a variety of ways throughout this collection. Sue Hubbell tells us how keeping bees has taught her to "pay attention in Springtime when the air feels electric and full of excitement." For a moment, when her "skin was tingling as the bees brushed past," she "felt almost part of the swarm." Annie Dillard shares a similar reaction when thousands of grasshoppers surround her in a meadow one summer evening; she was, she writes, "up to my knees in the world."

While it is difficult to categorize these twenty writers, some similar objectives are apparent. In each essay, the writer describes a place she finds personally enriching and ecologically intriguing. She is concerned about living compatibly with the land and learning as much as she can about her surroundings. Undoubtedly, her interest in nature generates unusual lifestyle choices and personal history.

For many of these women, writing about nature is an extension of their life's work. When Gretel Ehrlich learned to herd sheep, she was also learning about the landscape of Wyoming. Rachel Carson's descriptions of ocean life reflect her training as a marine biologist. And naturalist Hope Ryden's writings are a product of her studies of animal behavior and habitat.

Whatever their interest and training, they all share one occupation: Writing. Only a few writers presented here are not traditionally considered nature writers, specifically, the poet Maxine Kumin or the novelist Ursula K. Le Guin. Nonetheless, their essays and journals speak directly to human experience within the natural world, and their contributions provide important variations on nature writing themes.

Some of the writing collected here has been neglected and should enjoy a wider public forum. This is particularly so with the nineteenth-century writer Susan Fenimore Cooper, whose *Rural Hours* (1850) was immensely popular in America and England. Published four years before Thoreau's *Walden*, her journal reflections on Lake Otsego, New York, were the first of their kind to be published by a woman. Cooper's work reflects her belief in stewardship of the land, a rather long-sighted view considering America's expansionist and exploitative mood during the nineteenth century. She offers an important woman's perspective on nature at a time when men's experiences were more widely published.

Nature writing in America has been traditionally focused on men's experiences as explorers, scientists and naturalists, and policy makers throughout the course of American history. While these perspectives are important ones, I offer in this collection some additional voices and visions. America's natural history writing includes a diverse collection of experiences and knowledge; the many fine women writers presented here provide a view of women's evolving relationship with the natural world over the past two centuries.

Men and women writing about the land concern themselves with many of the same themes, and modern writers tend to consider the landscape simply as an entity into itself, with gender issues placed aside. However, the nineteenth- and early twentieth-century women writers are more fully aware of being women alone in the wilderness, perhaps because their activities were socially nontraditional. One notable difference between the writing of men and women is the absence in women's writing of "Land-as-

Woman" imagery concerned with the conquest and subjugation of the "virgin" land so evident in much of the early nature writing by men.

Two modern essays, in particular, defy the traditional image of nature as a woman to be tamed. Ursula K. Le Guin, in "A Very Warm Mountain" (1980), describes the erupting Mount St. Helens as a sister—not a mother. The sister is powerful, spewing "dirt and smoke and steam. She blackened half her face…like an angry brat." Leslie Marmon Silko explains that earth is "Mother Creator" in Pueblo history and myth. She is a powerful, dynamic spirit integral to the landscape. Both essays offer alternative ways of thinking about the natural world—an emphasis on bonding between humans and the landscape rather than on viewing the earth as an opposing force that must be subdued.

Le Guin shows us another side to the image of woman as an "indoor creature." As she recuperates at home from surgery, she has a good view of the erupting Mount St. Helens, 45 miles away. No idle observer, she notes the volcano's activities in her journal and remarks on its influence on the human psyche, revealing a spectrum of responses from the humans who "take it personally."

Also taking advantage of viewing nature from the comfort of her living room chair, Sue Hubbell spends one evening watching hundreds of tiny peep frogs suction themselves to her full-length windows, attracted by the light. This unexpected adventure causes her to investigate frog behavior—inside and outside the house.

Both women experience the good fortune of having the best seat in the house. Their essays are fascinating indoor observations.

The finest nature writing—both women's and men's—engages our imagination through its use of imagery. By creating images of daily life, of art, and of childhood in their writing, nature writers reveal as much about themselves as they do about their response to the landscape.

Ann Zwinger, a homemaker and naturalist, is "anxious to set up desert housekeeping, ready to begin these days of immaculate isolation" in the Sonoran Desert where heat "lies heavy as a mohair wool blanket." The daughter of Kansas pioneers, May Wynne Lamb describes the Kuskokwim River in Alaska as making its own "Hibernal covering in much the same fashion as we would piece together a crazy quilt." Diana Kappel-Smith, who lived in Vermont with her young son, sees trees "plastered with slush as though they were wearing bulky gray socks," and draws sap through tubes "hitched together with clamps and widgets like a giant set of Tinkertoys." And poet Maxine Kumin writes that a filly "shines, like a simonized Jaguar" and "moves the way a poem ought to move, once it's crafted."

One of the strongest elements of all nature writing is its treatment of environmental issues. Throughout this collection, these writers' respect for the land is evident in their emphasis on land and wildlife conservation issues.

Human intrusion is noted in several essays. Susan Fenimore Cooper sets the tone, as early as 1850, by condemning the clear-cutting of the forest near her village—the place where she regularly walked—and reprimanding those who "act so wastefully." Gretel Ehrlich finds Spam cans, the "tin-bright litter" left behind on a Wyoming ridge by other sheepherders, and oil wells that serve as fake "ridge-top jewelry." Hope Ryden's protectiveness of the beaver family she observes for four years has much to do with their history of near-extinction.

Beyond their vivid styles and discussion of issues, the writers reflect on two general themes of place: land that is linked with family history, and land that is "discovered," often as a result of travel or the desire to move from familiar places. What seems to matter most to these writers is that they can identify with their surroundings and discover places that become part of their personal histories.

Landscape and family history is a central theme in Terry Tempest Williams's book *Refuge: An Unnatural History of Family and Place* (1991). Great Salt Lake and the Utah desert are intertwined with her Mormon ancestry and her family's own sense of place; in a time of family loss, the land is a "refuge," a place of comfort in which she renews her strength. Leslie Marmon Silko writes eloquently of the New Mexico high desert and the importance it holds for her family and in her clan history. Both essays show how generational memories create a significant bond within human and natural history.

Nineteenth-century writers established strong family links to the land, as well. Susan Fenimore Cooper and Celia Thaxter both devoted much energy to preserving the land they had known since childhood. In many ways, they defined their adult life by these same places.

Susan Fenimore Cooper's journal writing demonstrates her familiarity with the New York woodlands, a familiarity that came from decades of living in the village founded by her grandfather. Her father, the novelist James Fenimore Cooper, undoubtedly influenced her sense of place through his novels such as *The Last of the Mohicans* (1826), part of the Leatherstocking Tales he wrote about frontier life. Stewardship of the land was Susan Cooper's talent: she deftly measures fallen trees with her parasol and jots down the circumference of a grapevine. The grander spots in other landscapes hold no appeal. Instead, she favors the simplicity of her home, "the quiet brook running through a meadow in some familiar spot."

Celia Thaxter, a poet, shares Cooper's view of stewardship. She lived most of her life on Appledore Island, off the coast of New Hampshire, where her family owned a summer resort. As the daughter of a lighthouse keeper, Thaxter's childhood was a lesson in island folklore, the yearly patterns of bird migrations, ocean storms, and plant and animal life. Thaxter's essays note changes in the island terrain, and she is familiar enough with loon behavior to understand when their haunting cries—"a shudder of sound"—warn of offshore storms. Her natural history knowledge came from years of observing her island home.

Some nineteenth-century women left their homelands and went in search of new terrain. The open spaces of the western frontier stirred their desire to explore unfamiliar landscapes; and, as they moved away from familiar places, they increased their chances of living independently, with fewer social restrictions. Such nontraditional lifestyles not only raised eyebrows but also inspired some intriguing nature writing!

Isabella Bird, who explored the Colorado Rockies in the 1870s when she was in her thirties, lived a dramatically different life for a woman of her time. Bird often travelled as a remedy for ill health and was on her way back to England from Hawaii when she stopped in Colorado. During the fall and winter of 1873, she travelled in the mountains on horseback, unarmed and often alone, much to the amazement of the local residents. Bird lived a long life—she was seventy-three when she died, but her illness created an excuse for travel (and adventure) away from her home in England. The mountains with their "life giving" air excited her appreciation both for natural beauty and personal freedom.

Thirty-seven years later, women travelling alone into the wilderness still had to maneuver social obstacles. May Wynne Lamb, the daughter of Welsh pioneers who had settled in Kansas, left for Alaska in 1916 to teach at a government school in a remote village on the Kuskokwim River. She was seventeen. During her voyage, Lamb was asked repeatedly why a single woman would choose to live in Alaska; many advised her to stay home and "associate with decent women." But Lamb loved to travel and wanted to follow in her pioneering mother's footsteps. Alaska's "final frontier" beckoned. As one of the few early records of women settlers, her writing portrays respectful admiration of the Kuskokwim River's magnificent beauty and force, and her own adaptation to the challenging arctic world.

Marjorie Kinnan Rawlings also faced similar social disapproval when she left the northeast and her journalism career in the late 1920s to farm an orange grove in Florida. Ignoring criticism, she lived independently at Cross Creek and discovered in the land both personal and literary inspiration; in fact, her Pulitzer Prize–winning novel *The Yearling* is based on the people and terrain of Cross Creek.

Rawlings, Lamb, and Bird made unusual choices for women of their times. By adapting to the challenge of wilderness living and accepting its discomforts, they were able to redefine their lives. Their writing underscores their delight in living harmoniously with nature.

By the middle of the twentieth century, it was less unusual for a woman to choose to live in a wilderness area. Several modern writers discover that moving to an unfamiliar place changes their lives for the better. Landscape becomes "home," a place of solace and restoration.

While rural living often has been romanticized in literature and in life, such sentimentality is absent from these women's essays. Integration with their surroundings is stressed more than discovery of place. This is evident in Helen Hoover's essay on living in the Minnesotan wilderness with her husband in the 1950s, well before the "back-to-the-land" movement. She writes crisply, "Nature does not coddle the weak," and learns from the animals living around her cabin when to begin preparing for the isolated winters.

Sue Hubbell frankly acknowledges that living alone on a southern Missouri farm was not her original intent. But she stayed on after she divorced and, while puzzling out some personal questions, slowly begins to rebuild her life. Note how nature assists in that process: "As I began to botanize, to learn to call the plants around me up here on my hill by their Latin names, I was diverted from my lack of wits by the wit of the system."

While the natural world can teach us how to survive, it can also provide solace, as it does for Gretel Ehrlich. In 1976, while making a film in Wyoming, Ehrlich was devastated by the death of a man she loved. She ultimately chooses to live in Wyoming, a place where she leads a rather solitary life amid ranchers and cowboys. The first time she herds sheep alone is a lesson in making decisions and learning to read the landscape—and her heart.

Beyond where and how they live, these writers emphasize the discoveries that come from paying close attention to the natural world. They are willing students of nature, seeking insight into the mysteries of the landscape.

New experiences are a priority for them. Often, this means returning again and again to the same familiar place. If they watch and listen attentively, they discover something unusual. Patience is required, however. Naturalist Hope Ryden, who studies a beaver family in Harriman State Park, New York, for four years, demonstrates patience by sitting through a snowstorm to see if the animals will emerge from their winter lodge.

Curiosity is a key factor in the discoveries they make, and they ask plenty of questions. How do maple trees know when to release their sap each spring? asks Diana Kappel-Smith. Even though she never discovers why, exactly, her imaginative role playing gives us a new perspective of sugar maple trees in springtime.

Discovery may also involve danger. As Ann Zwinger counts bighorn sheep in the Sonoran Desert, she nearly stumbles across a gila monster, a "fearsome-looking," venomous lizard usually hidden during the day. Regardless of the hazards, she enjoys camping in the desert, feels honored by the sheep's presence, and relishes the adventure. Where else can you measure your mettle against sunstroke and lizards?

But you needn't camp out in the desert to learn about nature's surprises. Danger can occur just as unexpectedly in your own backyard, as Mary Leister notes in her piece about a January fog that envelops her during a casual walk through the marsh. The fog is so thick it tests her ability to find her way home, but she is more interested in the intriguing surprise of the "thick-clustered fur of fine, long needles, crystal white" that the fog leaves behind on the goldenrod and thistle stalks.

Whether they are in familiar or unfamiliar surroundings, these writers are remarkably honest about their vulnerability in the landscape. Terry Tempest Williams writes that the "hostility" of the Utah desert teaches her "how to be quiet and unobtrusive, how to find grace among spiders with a poisonous bite." Yet, she will still "curl up in the grasses like a bedded animal and dream." Isabella Bird, climbing Longs Peak in 1873, feels humiliated because her guide, "Mountain Jim," insists on dragging her up part of the final ascent. Terror does not diminish her appreciation for the beauty of "mountain, canyon, and lake, sleeping in depths of blue and purple most ravishing to the eye." In fact, terror burns into her memory the "never-to-be-forgotten glories" of the mountain and she faces the descent of 3,500 feet "without a shiver."

These writers share with us their unique perspectives on the land as they search out the meaning of the natural world and their relationship with it. Because they wish to understand the natural world, it is, as Rachel Carson writes so beautifully, "the elusiveness of that meaning that haunts us, that sends us again and again into the natural world where the key to the riddle is hidden."

SUSAN FENIMORE COOPER
(1813–1894)

Susan Fenimore Cooper's Rural Hours *(1887) is one of the earliest nature collections written by a woman. These seasonal descriptions of the Otsego Lake area in New York were first published in 1850, four years before Thoreau's* Walden, *and revised in 1887 after thirty years of popularity in America and England. Her writing appealed to a wide audience because of its descriptions of rural America and the botanical information on the plants and flowers of the Lake Otsego area. She knew this land well, having lived most of her life in Cooperstown, a village founded by her grandfather. Although Cooper spent most of her time as a copyist for her father, the novelist James Fenimore Cooper, her writing and editing career included the novel* Elinor Wylie *(1846),* Worthy Women of our First Century *(1887), and the prefaces to her father's work.*

The following journal selections from Rural Hours *show Cooper as a self-appointed steward of the land; she likes to measure and take stock of even the most subtle changes in the forest. Most importantly, she denounces the practice of clear-cutting, a long-sighted view of conservation during a time when expansionism was favored.*

From *Rural Hours*

TUESDAY, MAY 16TH— Warm, cloudy day. The weather clears slowly, but the air is delightful, so soft and bland. Strolled away from the village in quiet fields by the river, where sloping meadows and a border of wood shut one out from the world. Sweetly calm; nothing stirring but the river flowing gently past, and a few solitary birds flitting quietly to and fro, like messengers of peace. The sunshine is scarcely needed to enhance the beauty of May. The veil of a cloudy sky seems, this evening, to throw an additional charm over the sweetness of the season. . .

Coming home through the fields, we found an old pine stretched its entire length on the grass; it must have lain there for years, slowly mouldering away, for it was decayed throughout and fallen asunder in many places, so as to follow the curving surface of the ground, but the whole line was entire, and measuring it with a parasol, we

9

made its height to be more than an hundred feet, although something was wanting at the summit. Its diameter, without the bark, was less than two feet.

Saturday, June 9th— Charming day. Pleasant row on the lake, which looks very inviting this warm weather; the views are always pleasing: hills and forest, farms and groves, encircling a beautiful sheet of water.

There is certainly no natural object, among all those which make up a landscape, winning so much upon our affection as water. It is an essential part of prospects widely different in character. Mountains form a more striking and imposing feature, and they give to a country a character of majesty which cannot exist without them; but not even the mountains, with all their sublime prerogative, can wholly satisfy the mind, when stripped of torrent, cascade, or lake; while, on the other hand, if there be only a quiet brook running through a meadow in some familiar spot, the eye will often turn, unconsciously, in that direction, and linger with interest upon the humble stream. Observe, also, that the waters in themselves are capable of the highest degree of beauty, without the aid of any foreign element to enhance their dignity; give them full sway, let them spread themselves into their wildest expanse, let them roll into boundless seas, enfolding the earth in their embrace, with half the heavens for their canopy, and assuredly they have no need to borrow from the mountain or the forest.

Our own highland lake can lay no claim to grandeur; it has no broad expanse, and the hills about cannot boast of any great height, yet there is a harmony in the different parts of the picture which gives it much merit, and which must always excite a lively feeling of pleasure. The hills are a charming setting for the lake at their feet, neither so lofty as to belittle the sheet of water, nor so low as to be tame and commonplace; there is abundance of wood on their swelling ridges to give the charm of forest scenery, enough of tillage to add the varied interest of cultivation; the lake, with its clear, placid waters, lies gracefully beneath the mountains, flowing here into a quiet little bay, there skirting a wooded point, filling its ample basin, without encroaching on its banks by a rood of marsh or bog.

Saturday, July 28th— In these times, the hewers of wood are an unsparing race. The first colonists looked upon a tree as an enemy, and to judge from appearances, one would think that something of the same spirit prevails among their descendants at the present hour. It is not surprising, perhaps, that a man whose chief object in life is to make money should turn his timber into bank-notes with all possible speed; but it is remarkable that any one at all aware of the value of wood, should act so wastefully as most men do in this part of the world. Mature trees, young saplings, and last year's seedlings, are all destroyed at one blow by the axe or by fire; the spot where they have stood is left, perhaps, for a lifetime without any attempt at cultivation, or any endeavor to foster new wood. One would think that by this time, when the forest has fallen in all the valleys— when the hills are becoming more bare every day—when timber and fuel are rising in prices, and new uses are found for even indifferent woods—some forethought and care in this respect would be natural in people laying claim to common sense. . . .

How easy it would be to improve most of the farms in the country by a little attention to the woods and trees, improving their appearance, and adding to their market value at the same time! Thinning woods and not blasting them; clearing only such ground as is marked for immediate tillage; preserving the wood on the hill-tops and rough side-hills; encouraging a coppice on this or that knoll; permitting bushes and young trees to grow at will along the brooks and water-courses; sowing, if need be, a grove on the bank of the pool, such as are found on many of our farms; sparing an elm or two about the spring, with a willow also to overhang the well; planting one or two chestnuts, or oaks, or beeches, near the gates or bars; leaving a few others scattered about every field to shade the cattle in summer, as is frequently done, and setting out others in groups, or singly, to shade the house—how little would be the labor or expense required to accomplish all this, and how desirable would be the result! Assuredly, the pleasing character thus given to a farm and a neighborhood is far from being beneath the consideration of a sensible man. . . .

Thursday, August 24th—Brilliant day. Passed the afternoon on the lake. The views were very beautiful. Downy seeds of various kinds, thistle, dandelion, etc., etc., were thickly strewed over the bosom of the lake; we had never before observed such numbers of them lying on the water.

Saw a crane of the largest size flying over the lake, a mile or two to the northward of our boat. A pair of them have been about the lake all summer; they are said to be the large brown crane. We found one of their young this afternoon lying dead upon the bank of a brook, to which we gave the name of Crane Brook on this occasion. It was a good-sized bird, and seemed to have been killed in a fight with some winged enemy, for it had not been shot. As for the boldness of calling the brook after it, the pretty little stream had no name before; why not give it one?

Last summer a pair of eagles built their nest on one of the western hills, which we ventured to call Eagle Hill, on the same principle. These noble birds are occasionally seen hovering over the valley, though not often.

Measured an old grape-vine in the glen, near Crane Brook; it proved to be seven inches in circumference.

Thursday, September 21st—Equinox. Warm; showery as April. Sunshine, showers, and rainbows succeeding each other through the day. Beautiful effect of light on the hills; a whole mountain side on the lake shore bathed in the tints of the rainbow, the colors lying with unusual breadth on its wooded breast. Even the ethereal green of the bow was clearly seen above the darker verdure of the trees. Only the lower part of the bow, that which lay upon the mountain, was colored; above, the clouds were just tinged where they touched the brow of the hill, then fading away into pale gray.

Wednesday, February 28th—It is an additional charm of these clear, mild days in winter, that they often bring very beautiful sunsets. Not those gorgeous piles of clouds which are seen, perhaps, as frequently after the summer showers, as at any other period; but the sort of sunset one would not look for in winter—some of the softest and sweetest skies of the year. This evening the heavens were very beautiful, as we drove homeward over the ice; and the same effect may frequently be seen in December, January, or February. One of the most beautiful sunsets I have ever beheld occurred here several years since, toward the last of February. At such times, a warmer sun than usual draws from the yielding snow a mild mist, which softens the dark hills, and rising to the sky, lies there in long, light, cloudy folds. The choicest tints of the heavens are seen at such moments; tender shades of rose, lilac, and warm gold, opening to show beyond a sky filled with delicate green light. . . .

Isabella Bird
(1831–1904)

While exploring the Colorado Rocky Mountains during the autumn and winter of 1873, Isabella Bird defied below-freezing temperatures and kept her ink bottle warm enough to write letters to her sister in England. These lively accounts of the landscape and the people she encountered were published in A Lady's Life in the Rocky Mountains *(1879). Bird, who travelled away from her home in Yorkshire, England, in search of better health, ascended Longs Peak in Colorado only five years after the first ascent by the famous explorer John Wesley Powell. She clearly enjoyed the freedom of travelling the Rockies on horseback, often alone, over difficult, snow-covered terrain. This letter vividly narrates her ascent of Longs Peak with her guide "Mountain Jim." It reveals some terrifying moments, as well as the beautiful wilderness that was more than she "dared to hope for."*

"Estes Park, Colorado, October"

AS THIS ACCOUNT of the ascent of Long's Peak could not be written at the time, I am much disinclined to write it, especially as no sort of description within my powers could enable another to realize the glorious sublimity, the majestic solitude, and the unspeakable awfulness and fascination of the scenes in which I spent Monday, Tuesday, and Wednesday.

Long's Peak, 14,700 feet high, blocks up one end of Estes Park, and dwarfs all the surrounding mountains. From it on this side rise, snow-born, the bright St. Vrain, and the Big and Little Thompson. By sunlight or moonlight its splintered grey crest is the one object which, in spite of wapiti and bighorn, skunk and grizzly, unfailingly arrests the eyes. From it come all storms of snow and wind, and the forked lightnings play round its head like a glory. It is one of the noblest of mountains, but in one's imagination it grows to be much more than a mountain. It becomes invested with a personality. In its caverns and abysses one comes to fancy that it generates and chains the strong winds, to let them loose in its fury. The thunder becomes its voice, and the lightnings do it homage. Other summits blush under the morning kiss of the sun, and turn pale the next moment; but it detains the first sunlight and holds it round its head for an hour at least, till it pleases to change from rosy red to deep blue; and the sunset, as if spell-bound, lingers latest on its crest. The soft winds which hardly rustle the pine needles down here are raging rudely up there round its motionless summit. The mark of fire is upon it; and though it has passed into a grim repose, it tells of fire and upheaval as truly, though not as eloquently, as the living volcanoes of Hawaii. Here under its shadow one learns how naturally nature worship, and the propitiation of the forces of nature, arose in minds which had no better light.

Long's Peak, "the American Matterhorn," as some call it, was ascended five years ago for the first time. I thought I should like to attempt it, but up to Monday, when Evans left for Denver, cold water was thrown upon the project. It was too late in the season, the winds were likely to be strong, etc.; but just before leaving, Evans said that the weather was looking more settled, and if I did not get farther than the timber line it would be worth going. Soon after he left, "Mountain Jim" came in, and he would go up as guide, and the two youths who rode here with me from Longmount and I caught at the proposal. Mrs. Edwards at once baked bread for three days, steaks were cut from the steer which hangs up conveniently, and tea, sugar, and butter were benevolently added. Our picnic was not to be a luxurious or "well-found" one, for, in order to avoid the expense of a pack mule, we limited our luggage to what our saddle horses could carry. Behind my saddle I carried three pair of camping blankets and a quilt, which reached to my shoulders. My own boots were so much worn that it was painful to walk, even about the park, in them, so Evans had lent me a pair of his hunting boots, which hung to the horn of my saddle. The horses of the two young men were equally loaded, for we had to prepare for many degrees of frost. "Jim" was a shocking figure; he had on an old pair of high boots, with a baggy pair of old trousers made of deer hide, held on by an old scarf tucked into them; a leather shirt, with three or four ragged unbuttoned waistcoats over it; an old smashed wideawake, from under which his tawny, neglected ringlets hung; and with his one eye, his one long spur, his knife in his belt, his revolver in his waistcoat pocket, his saddle covered with an old beaver skin, from which the paws hung down; his camping blankets behind him, his rifle laid across the saddle in front of him, and his axe, canteen, and other gear hanging to the horn, he was as awful-looking a ruffian as one could see. By way of contrast he rode a small Arab mare, of exquisite beauty, skittish, high spirited, gentle, but altogether too light for him, and he fretted her incessantly to make her display herself.

Heavily loaded as all our horses were, "Jim" started over the half-mile of level grass at a hard gallop, and then throwing his mare on her haunches, pulled up alongside of me, and with a grace of manner which soon made me forget his appearance, entered into a conversation which lasted for more than three hours, in spite of the manifold checks of fording streams, single file, abrupt ascents and descents, and other incidents of mountain travel. The ride was one series of glories and surprises, of "park" and glade, of lake and stream, of mountains on mountains, culminating in the rent pinnacles of Long's Peak, which looked yet grander and ghastlier as we crossed an attendant mountain 11,000 feet high. The slanting sun added fresh beauty every hour. There were dark pines against a lemon sky, grey peaks reddening and etherealizing, gorges of deep and infinite blue, floods of golden glory pouring through canyons of enormous depth, an atmosphere of absolute purity, an occasional foreground of cotton-wood and aspen flaunting in red and gold to intensify the blue gloom of the pines, the trickle and murmur of streams fringed with icicles, the strange *sough* of gusts moving among the pine-tops—sights and sounds not of the lower earth, but of the solitary, beast-haunted, frozen upper altitudes. From the dry, buff grass of Estes Park we turned off up a trail on the side of a pine-hung gorge, up a steep pine-clothed hill, down to a small valley, rich in fine, sun-cured hay about eighteen inches high, and enclosed by high mountains whose deepest hollow contains a lily-covered lake, fitly named "The Lake of the Lilies." Ah, how magical its beauty was, as it slept in silence, where *there* the dark pines were mirrored motionless in its pale gold, and *here* the great white lily cups and dark green leaves rested on amethyst-colored water!

From this we ascended into the purple gloom of great pine forests which clothe the skirts of the mountains up to a height of about 11,000 feet, and from their chill and solitary depths we had glimpses of golden atmosphere and rose-lit summits, not of "the land very far off," but of the land nearer now in all its grandeur, gaining in sublimity by nearness—glimpses, too, through a broken vista of purple gorges, of the illimitable Plains lying idealized in the late sunlight, their baked, brown expanse transfigured into the likeness of a sunset sea rolling infinitely in waves of misty gold.

We rode upwards through the gloom on a steep trail blazed through the forest, all my intellect concentrated on avoiding being dragged off my horse by impending branches, or having the blankets badly torn, as those of my companions were, by sharp dead limbs, between which there was hardly room to pass—the horses breathless, and requiring to stop every few yards, though their riders, except myself, were afoot. The gloom of the dense, ancient, silent forest is to me awe inspiring. On such an evening it is soundless, except for the branches creaking in the soft wind, the frequent snap of decayed timber, and a murmur in the pine tops as of a not distant waterfall, all tending to produce *eeriness* and a sadness "hardly akin to pain." There no lumberer's axe has ever rung. The trees die when they have attained their prime, and stand there, dead and bare, till the fierce mountain winds lay them prostrate. The pines grew smaller and more sparse as we ascended, and the last stragglers wore a tortured, warring look. The timber line was passed, but yet a little higher a slope of mountain meadow dipped to the south-west towards a bright stream trickling under ice and icicles, and there a grove of the beautiful silver spruce marked our camping ground. The trees were in miniature, but so exquisitely arranged that one might well ask what artist's hand had planted them, scattering them here, clumping them there, and training their slim spires towards heaven. Hereafter, when I call up memories of the glorious, the view from this camping ground will come up. Looking east, gorges opened to the distant Plains, then fading into purple grey. Mountains with pine-clothed skirts rose in ranges, or, solitary, uplifted their grey summits, while close behind, but nearly 3,000 feet above us, towered the bald white crest of Long's Peak, its huge precipices red with the light of a sun long lost to our eyes. Close to us, in the caverned side of the Peak, was snow that, owing to its position, is eternal. Soon the afterglow came on, and before it faded a big half-moon hung out of the heavens, shining through the silver blue foliage of the pines on the frigid background of snow, and turning the whole into fairyland. The "photo" which accompanies this letter is by a courageous Denver artist who attempted the ascent just before I arrived, but, after camping out at the timber line for a week, was foiled by the perpetual storms, and was driven down again, leaving some very valuable apparatus about 3,000 feet from the summit.

Unsaddling and picketing the horses securely, making the beds of pine shoots, and dragging up logs for fuel, warmed us all. "Jim" built up a great fire, and before long we were all sitting around it at supper. It didn't matter much that we had to drink our tea out of the battered meat tins in which it was boiled, and eat strips of beef reeking with pine smoke without plates or forks.

"Treat Jim as a gentleman and you'll find him one," I had been told; and though his manner was certainly bolder and freer than that of gentlemen generally, no imaginary fault could be found. He was very agreeable as a man of culture as well as a child of nature; the desperado was altogether out of sight. He was very courteous and even kind to me, which was fortunate, as the young men had little idea of showing even ordinary civilities. That night I made the acquaintance of his dog "Ring," said to be the best hunting dog in Colorado, with the body and legs of a collie, but a head approaching that of a mastiff, a noble face with a wistful human expression, and the most truthful eyes I ever saw in an animal. His master loves him if he loves anything, but in his savage moods ill-treats him. "Ring's" devotion never swerves, and his truthful eyes are rarely taken off his master's face. He is almost human in his intelligence, and, unless he is told to do so, he never takes notice of any one but "Jim." In a tone as if speaking to a human being, his master, pointing to me, said, "Ring, go to that lady, and don't leave her again to-night." "Ring" at once came to me, looked into my face, laid his head on my shoulder, and then lay down beside me with his head on my lap, but never taking his eyes from "Jim's" face.

The long shadows of the pines lay upon the frosted grass, an aurora leaped fitfully, and the moonlight, though intensely bright, was pale beside the red, leaping flames of our pine logs and their red glow on our gear, ourselves, and Ring's truthful face. One of the young men sang a Latin student's song and two Negro melodies; the other "Sweet Spirit, hear my Prayer." "Jim" sang one of Moore's melodies in a singular falsetto, and all together sang, "The Star-spangled Banner" and "The Red, White, and Blue." Then "Jim" recited a very clever poem of his own composition, and told some fearful Indian stories. A group of small silver spruces away from the fire was my sleeping place. The artist who had been up there had so woven and interlaced their lower branches as to form a bower, affording at once shelter from the wind and a most agreeable privacy. It was thickly strewn with young pine shoots, and these, when covered with a blanket, with an inverted saddle for a pillow, made a luxurious bed. The mercury at 9 P.M. was 12° below the freezing point. "Jim," after a last look at the horses, made a huge fire, and stretched himself out beside it, but "Ring" lay at my back to keep me warm. I could not sleep, but the night passed rapidly. I was anxious about the ascent, for gusts of ominous sound swept through the pines at intervals. Then wild animals howled, and "Ring" was perturbed in spirit about them. Then it was strange to see the notorious desperado, a red-handed man, sleeping as quietly as innocence sleeps. But, above all, it was exciting to lie there, with no better shelter than a bower of pines, on a mountain 11,000 feet high, in the very heart of the Rocky Range, under twelve degrees of frost, hearing sounds of wolves, with shivering stars looking through the fragrant canopy, with arrowy pines for bed-posts, and for a night lamp the red flames of a camp-fire.

Day dawned long before the sun rose, pure and lemon colored. The rest were looking after the horses, when one of the students came running to tell me that I must come farther down the slope, for "Jim" said he had never seen such a sunrise. From the chill, grey Peak above, from the everlasting snows, from the silvered pines, down through mountain ranges with their depths of Tyrian purple, we looked to where the Plains lay cold, in blue-grey, like a morning sea against a far horizon. Suddenly, as a dazzling streak at first, but enlarging rapidly into a dazzling sphere, the sun wheeled above the grey line, a light and glory as when it was first created. "Jim" involuntarily and reverently uncovered his head, and exclaimed, "I believe there is a God!" I felt as if, Parsee-like, I must worship. The grey of the Plains changed to purple, the sky was all one rose-red flush, on which vermilion cloud-streaks rested; the ghastly peaks gleamed like rubies, the earth and heavens were newly created. Surely "the Most High dwelleth not in temples made with hands!" For a full hour those Plains simulated the ocean, down to whose limitless expanse of purple, cliff, rocks, and promontories swept down.

By seven we had finished breakfast, and passed into the ghastlier solitudes above, I riding as far as what, rightly or wrongly, are called the "Lava Beds," an expanse of large and small boulders, with snow in their crevices. It was very cold; some water which we crossed was frozen hard enough to bear the horse. "Jim" had advised me against taking any wraps, and my thin Hawaiian riding dress, only fit for the tropics, was penetrated by the keen air. The rarefied atmosphere soon began to oppress our breathing, and I found that Evans's boots were so large that I had no foothold. Fortunately, before the real difficulty of the ascent began, we found, under a rock, a pair of small overshoes, probably left by the Hayden exploring expedition, which just lasted for the day. As we were leaping from rock to rock, "Jim" said, "I was thinking in the night about your traveling alone, and wondering where you carried your Derringer, for I could see no signs of it." On my telling him that I traveled unarmed, he could hardly believe it, and adjured me to get a revolver at once.

On arriving at the "Notch" (a literal gate of rock), we found ourselves absolutely on the knifelike ridge or backbone of Long's Peak, only a few feet wide, covered with colossal boulders and fragments, and on the other side shelving in one precipitous, snow-patched sweep of 3,000 feet to a picturesque hollow, containing a lake of pure green water. Other lakes, hidden among dense pine woods, were farther off, while close above us rose the Peak, which, for about 500 feet, is a smooth, gaunt, inaccessible-looking pile of granite. Passing through the "Notch," we looked along the nearly inaccessible side of the Peak, composed of boulders and *debris* of all shapes and sizes, through which appeared broad, smooth ribs of reddish-colored granite, looking as if they upheld the towering rock mass above. I usually dislike bird's-eye and panoramic views, but, though from a mountain, this was not one. Serrated ridges, not much lower than that on which we stood, rose, one beyond another, far as that pure atmosphere could carry the vision, broken into awful chasms deep with ice and snow, rising into pinnacles piercing the heavenly blue with their cold, barren grey, on, on for ever, till the most distant range upbore unsullied snow alone. There were fair lakes mirroring the dark pine woods, canyons dark and blue-black with unbroken expanses of pines, snow-slashed pinnacles, wintry heights frowning upon lovely parks, watered and wooded, lying in the lap of summer; North Park floating off into the blue distance, Middle Park closed till another season, the sunny slopes of Estes Park, and winding down among the mountains the snowy ridge of the Divide, whose bright waters seek both the Atlantic and Pacific Oceans. There, far below, links of diamonds showed where the Grand River takes its rise to seek the mysterious Colorado, with its still unsolved enigma, and lose itself in the waters of the Pacific; and nearer the snow-born Thompson bursts forth from the ice to begin its journey to the Gulf of Mexico. Nature, rioting in her grandest mood, exclaimed with voices of grandeur, solitude, sublimity, beauty, and infinity, "Lord, what is man, that Thou art mindful of him? or the son of man, that Thou visitest him?" Never-to-be-forgotten glories they were, burnt in upon my memory by six succeeding hours of terror.

You know I have no head and no ankles, and never ought to dream of mountaineering; and had I known that the ascent was a real mountaineering feat I should not have felt the slightest ambition to perform it. As it is, I am only humiliated by my success, for "Jim" dragged me up, like a bale of goods, by sheer force of muscle. At the "Notch" the real business of the ascent began. Two thousand feet of solid rock towered above us, four thousand feet of broken rock shelved precipitously below; smooth granite ribs, with barely foothold, stood out here and there; melted snow refrozen several times, presented a more serious obstacle; many of the rocks were loose, and tumbled down when touched. To me it was a time of extreme terror. I was roped to "Jim," but it was of no use; my feet were paralyzed and slipped on the bare rock, and he said it was useless to try to go that way, and we retraced our steps. I wanted to return to the "Notch," knowing that my incompetence would detain the party, and one of the young men said almost plainly that a woman was a dangerous encumbrance, but the trapper replied shortly that if it were not to take a lady up he would not go up at all. He went on the explore, and reported that further progress on the correct line of ascent was blocked by ice; and then for two hours we descended, lowering ourselves by our hands from rock to rock along a boulder-strewn sweep of 4,000 feet, patched with ice and snow, and perilous from rolling stones. My fatigue, giddiness, and pain from bruised ankles, and arms half pulled out of their sockets, were so great that I should never have gone half-way had not "Jim," *nolens volens*, dragged me along with a patience and skill, and withal a determination that I should ascend the Peak, which never failed. After descending about 2,000 feet to avoid the ice, we got into a deep ravine with inaccessible sides, partly filled with ice and snow and partly with large and small fragments of rock, which were constantly giving away, rendering the footing very insecure. That part to me was two hours of painful and unwilling submission to the inevitable; of trembling, slipping, straining, of smooth ice appearing when it was least expected, and of weak entreaties to be left behind while the others went on. "Jim" always said that there was no danger, that there was only a short bad bit ahead, and that I should go up even if he carried me!

Slipping, faltering, gasping from the exhausting toil in the rarefied air, with throbbing hearts and panting lungs, we reached the top of the gorge and squeezed ourselves between two gigantic fragments of rock by a passage called the "Dog's Lift," when I climbed on the shoulders of one man and then was hauled up. This introduced us by an abrupt turn round the south-west angle of the Peak to a narrow shelf of considerable length, rugged, uneven, and so overhung by the cliff in some places that it is necessary to crouch to pass at all. Above, the Peak looks nearly vertical for 400 feet; and below, the most tremendous precipice I have ever seen descends in one unbroken fall. This is usually considered the most dangerous part of the ascent, but it does not seem so to me, for such foothold as there is is secure, and one fancies that it is possible to hold on with the hands. But there, and on the final, and, to my thinking, the worst part of the climb, one slip, and a breathing, thinking, human being would lie 3,000 feet below, a shapeless, bloody heap! "Ring" refused to traverse the Ledge, and remained at the "Lift" howling piteously.

From thence the view is more magnificent even than that from the "Notch." At the foot of the precipice below us lay a lovely lake, wood embosomed, from or near which the bright St. Vrain and other streams take their rise. I thought how their clear cold waters, growing turbid in the affluent flats, would heat under the tropic sun, and eventually form part of that great ocean river which renders our far-off islands habitable by impinging on their shores. Snowy ranges, one behind the other, extended to the distant horizon, folding in their wintry embrace the beauties of Middle Park. Pike's Peak, more than one hundred miles off, lifted that vast but shapeless summit which is the landmark of southern Colorado. There were snow patches, snow slashes, snow abysses, snow forlorn and soiled looking, snow pure and dazzling, snow glistening above the purple robe of pine worn by all the mountains; while away to the east, in limitless breadth, stretched the green-grey of the endless Plains. Giants everywhere reared their splintered crests. From thence, with a single sweep, the eye takes in a distance of 300 miles—that distance to the west, north, and south being made up of mountains ten, eleven, twelve, and thirteen thousand feet in height, dominated by Long's Peak, Gray's Peak, and Pike's Peak, all nearly the height of Mont Blanc! On the Plains we traced the rivers by their fringe of cottonwoods to the distant Platte, and between us and them lay glories of mountain, canyon, and lake, sleeping in depths of blue and purple most ravishing to the eye.

As we crept from the ledge round a horn of rock I beheld what made me perfectly sick and dizzy to look at—the terminal Peak itself—a smooth, cracked face or wall of pink granite, as nearly perpendicular as anything could well be up which it was possible to climb, well deserving the name of the "American Matterhorn."[1]

Scaling, not climbing, is the correct term for this last ascent. It took one hour to accomplish 500 feet, pausing for breath every minute or two. The only foothold was in narrow cracks or on minute projections on the granite. To get a toe in these cracks, or

[1]Let no practical mountaineer be allured by my description into the ascent of Long's Peak. Truly terrible as it was to me, to a member of the Alpine Club it would not be a feat worth performing.

here and there on a scarcely obvious projection, while crawling on hands and knees, all the while tortured with thirst and gasping and struggling for breath, this was the climb; but at last the Peak was won. A grand, well-defined mountain top it is, a nearly level acre of boulders, with precipitous sides all round, the one we came up being the only accessible one.

It was not possible to remain long. One of the young men was seriously alarmed by bleeding from the lungs, and the intense dryness of the day and the rarefication of the air, at a height of nearly 15,000 feet, made respiration very painful. There is always water on the Peak, but it was frozen as hard as a rock, and the sucking of ice and snow increases thirst. We all suffered severely from the want of water, and the gasping for breath made our mouths and tongues so dry that articulation was difficult, and the speech of all unnatural.

From the summit were seen in unrivalled combination all the views which had rejoiced our eyes during the ascent. It was something at last to stand upon the storm-rent crown of this lonely sentinel of the Rocky Range, on one of the mightiest of the vertebrae of the backbone of the North American continent, and to see the waters start for both oceans. Uplifted above love and hate and storms of passion, calm amidst the eternal silences, fanned by zephyrs and bathed in living blue, peace rested for that one bright day on the Peak, as if it were some region

Where falls not rain, or hail, or any snow,
Or ever wind blows loudly.

We placed our names, with the date of ascent, in a tin within a crevice, and descended to the Ledge, sitting on the smooth granite, getting our feet into cracks and against projections, and letting ourselves down by our hands, "Jim" going before me, so that I might steady my feet against his powerful shoulders. I was no longer giddy, and faced the precipice of 3,500 feet without a shiver. Repassing the Ledge and Lift, we accomplished the descent through 1,500 feet of ice and snow, with many falls and bruises, but no worse mishap, and there separated, the young men taking the steepest but most direct way to the "Notch," with the intention of getting ready for the march home, and "Jim" and I taking what he thought the safer route for me—a descent over boulders for 2,000 feet, and then a tremendous ascent to the "Notch." I had various falls, and once hung by my frock, which caught on a rock, and "Jim" severed it with his hunting knife, upon which I fell into a crevice full of soft snow. We were driven lower down the mountains than he had intended by impassable tracts of ice, and the ascent was tremendous. For the last 200 feet the boulders were of enormous size, and the steepness fearful. Sometimes I drew myself up on hands and knees, sometimes crawled;

sometimes "Jim" pulled me up by my arms or a lariat, and sometimes I stood on his shoulders, or he made steps for me of his feet and hands, but at six we stood on the "Notch" in the splendor of the sinking sun, all color deepening, all peaks glorifying, all shadows purpling, all peril past.

"Jim" had parted with his *brusquerie* when we parted from the students, and was gentle and considerate beyond anything, though I knew that he must be grievously disappointed, both in my courage and strength. Water was an object of earnest desire. My tongue rattled in my mouth, and I could hardly articulate. It is good for one's sympathies to have for once a severe experience of thirst. Truly, there was

> *Water, water, everywhere,*
> *But not a drop to drink.*

Three times its apparent gleam deceived even the mountaineer's practised eye, but we found only a foot of "glare ice." At last, in a deep hole, he succeeded in breaking the ice, and by putting one's arm far down one could scoop up a little water in one's hand, but it was tormentingly insufficient. With great difficulty and much assistance I recrossed the "Lava Beds," was carried to the horse and lifted upon him, and when we reached the camping ground I was lifted off him, and laid on the ground wrapped up in blankets, a humiliating termination of a great exploit. The horses were saddled, and the young men were all ready to start, but "Jim" quietly said, "Now, gentlemen, I want a good night's rest, and we shan't stir from here to-night." I believe they were really glad to have it so, as one of them was quite "finished." I retired to my arbor, wrapped myself in a roll of blankets, and was soon asleep.

When I woke, the moon was high shining through the silvery branches, whitening the bald Peak above, and glittering on the great abyss of snow behind, and pine logs were blazing like a bonfire in the cold still air. My feet were so icy cold that I could not sleep again, and getting some blankets to sit in, and making a roll of them for my back, I sat for two hours by the camp-fire. It was weird and gloriously beautiful. The students were asleep not far off in their blankets with their feet towards the fire. "Ring" lay on one side of me with his fine head on my arm, and his master sat smoking, with the fire lighting up the handsome side of his face, and except for the tones of our voices, and an occasional crackle and splutter as a pine knot blazed up, there was no sound on the mountain side. The beloved stars of my far-off home were overhead, the Plough and Pole Star, with their steady light; the glittering Pleiades, looking larger than I ever saw them, and "Orion's studded belt" shining gloriously. Once only some wild animals prowled near the camp, when "Ring," with one bound, disappeared from my side; and the horses, which were picketed by the stream, broke their lariats, stampeded, and came rushing wildly toward the fire, and it was fully half an hour before they were caught and quiet was restored. "Jim," or Mr. Nugent, as I always scrupulously called him, told stories of his early youth, and of a great sorrow which had led him to embark on a lawless and desperate life. His voice trembled, and tears rolled down his cheek. Was it semi-conscious acting, I wondered, or was his dark soul really stirred to its depths by the silence, the beauty, and the memories of youth?

We reached Estes Park at noon of the following day. A more successful ascent of the Peak was never made, and I would not now exchange my memories of its perfect beauty and extraordinary sublimity for any other experience of mountaineering in any part of the world. Yesterday snow fell on the summit, and it will be inaccessible for eight months to come.

As the daughter of a lighthouse keeper, Celia Laighton Thaxter spent her childhood years on White Island, one of the isolated shoal islands nine miles off the coast of New Hampshire. In 1848, at the age of thirteen, Thaxter and her family moved to Appledore, the largest of the islands, where they ran a summer resort visited by such literary figures as Nathaniel Hawthorne, Henry Thoreau, Ralph Waldo Emerson, Childe Hassam, and Sarah Orne Jewett. Appledore Island was the subject of much of her writing, including her first poem "Landlocked," published in the Atlantic, *and the popular gardening book* An Island Garden *(1894).* Among the Isles of Shoals *(1873) portrays the natural history and folklore of the shoal islands. Thaxter's familiarity with the landscape is evident in the following selection, where she describes the warning signals that precede a dramatic ocean storm.*

From *Among the Isles of Shoals*

AND HERE THE LOONS CONGREGATE in spring and autumn. These birds seem to me the most human and at the same time the most demoniac of their kind. I learned to imitate their different cries; they are wonderful! At one time the loon language was so familiar that I could almost always summon a considerable flock by going down to the water and assuming the neighborly and conversational tone which they generally use: after calling a few minutes, first a far-off voice responded, then other voices answered him, and when this was kept up a while, half a dozen birds would come sailing in. It was the most delightful little party imaginable; so comical were they, so entertaining, that it was impossible not to laugh aloud,— and they could laugh too, in a way which chilled the marrow of one's bones. They always laugh, when shot at, if they are missed; as the Shoalers say, "They laugh like a warrior." But their long, wild, melancholy cry before a storm is the most awful note I ever heard from a bird. It is so sad, so hopeless—a clear, high shriek, shaken, as it drops into silence, into broken notes that make you think of the fluttering of a pennon in the wind—a shudder of sound. They invariably utter this cry before a storm.

Between the gales from all points of the compass, that

"'twixt the green sea and the azured vault
Set roaring war,"

some day there falls a dead calm; the whole expanse of the ocean is like a mirror; there's
not a whisper of a wave, not a sigh from any wind about the world—an awful, breathless pause prevails. Then if a loon swims into the motionless little bights about the
island, and raises his weird cry, the silent rocks re-echo the unearthly tone, and it seems
as if the crture were in league with the mysterious forces that are so soon to turn this
deathly stillness into confusion and dismay. All through the day the ominous quiet
lasts; in the afternoon, while yet the sea is glassy, a curious undertone of mournful
sound can be perceived—not fitful—a steady moan such as the wind makes over the
mouth of an empty jar. Then the islanders say, "Do you hear Hog Island crying? Now
look out for a storm!" No one knows how that low moaning is produced, or why
Appledore, of all the islands, should alone lament before the tempest. Through its
gorges, perhaps, some current of wind sighs with that hollow cry. Yet the sea could
hardly keep its unruffled surface were a wind abroad sufficient to draw out the boding
sound. Such a calm preceded the storm which destroyed the Minot's Ledge Lighthouse
in 1849. I never knew such silence. Though the sun blazed without a cloud, the sky and
sea were utterly wan and colorless, and before sunset the mysterious tone began to
vibrate in the breezeless air. "Hog Island's crying!" said the islanders. One could but
think of the Ancient Mariner, as the angry sun went down in a brassy glare, and still no
ripple broke the calm. But with the twilight gathered the waiting wind, slowly and
steadily; and before morning the shock of the breakers was like the incessant thunder-
ing of heavy guns; the solid rock perceptibly trembled; windows shook, and glass and
china rattled in the house. It is impossible to describe the confusion, the tumult, the
rush and roar and thunder of waves and wind overwhelming those rocks—the whole
Atlantic rushing headlong to cast itself upon them. It was very exciting: the most timid
among us lost all sense of fear. Before the next night the sea had made a breach through
the valley on Appledore, in which the houses stand—a thing that never had happened
within the memory of the oldest inhabitant. The waves piled in from the eastward
(where Old Harry was tossing the breakers sky-high)—a maddened troop of giants,
sweeping everything before them—and followed one another, white as milk, through
the valley from east to west, strewing the space with boulders from a solid wall six feet
high and as many thick, which ran across the top of the beach, and which one tremendous wave toppled over like a child's fence of blocks. Kelp and seaweed were piled in

banks high up along the shore, and strewed the doorsteps; and thousands of the hideous creatures known among the Shoalers as sea-mice, a holothurian (a livid, shapeless mass of torpid life), were scattered in all directions. While the storm was at its height, it was impossible to do anything but watch it through windows beaten by the blinding spray which burst in flying clouds all over the island, drenching every inch of the soil in foaming brine. In the coves the "yeasty surges" were churned into yellow masses of foam, that blew across in trembling flakes, and clung wherever they lit, leaving a hoary scum of salt when dry, which remained till sweet, fair water dropped out of the clouds to wash it all away. It was long before the sea went down; and, days after the sun began to shine, the fringe of spray still leaped skyward from the eastern shore, and Shag and Mingo Rocks at Duck Island tossed their distant clouds of snow against the blue.

After the wind subsided, it was curious to examine the effects of the breakers on the eastern shore, where huge masses of rock were struck off from the cliffs, and flung among the wild heaps of scattered boulders, to add to the already hopeless confusion of the gorges. The eastern aspects of the islands change somewhat every year or two from this cause; and, indeed, over all their surfaces continual change goes on from the action of the weather. Under the hammer and chisel of frost and heat, masses of stone are detached and fall from the edges of cliffs, whole ledges become disintegrated, the rock cracks in smooth, thin sheets, and, once loosened, the whole mass can be pulled out, sheet by sheet. Twenty years ago those subtle, irresistible tools of the weather had cracked off a large mass of rock from a ledge on the slope of a gentle declivity. I could just lay my hand in the space then: now three men can walk abreast between the ledge and the detached mass; and nothing has touched it save heat and cold. The whole aspect of the rocks is infinitely aged. I never can see the beautiful salutation of sunrise upon their hoary fronts, without thinking how many millions of times they have answered to that delicate touch....

MABEL OSGOOD WRIGHT
(1859–1934)

In The Friendship of Nature: A New England Chronicle of Birds and Flowers *(1894), Mabel Osgood Wright invites her readers to examine the nineteenth-century Connecticut countryside—the garden, fields, and forest surrounding her home. "A New England May-Day" illustrates a traditional style of nature writing for nineteenth-century women which emphasizes bird and flower descriptions embellished with literary references. Wright, an amateur ornithologist, was an editor for* Bird-Lore *and a founder of the Connecticut Audubon, and her writing reflects her knowledge of bird populations in nineteenth-century New England. This essay also demonstrates how her garden became a starting point for her exploration of the natural world.*

"A New England May-Day"

HERE IN NEW ENGLAND, we have no calendar of Nature, no rigid law of season, or of growth. The climate, a caprice, a wholly eerie thing, sets tradition at defiance and forces our poets to contradict each other. The flower which one declares the harbinger of spring may be a lazy vanguard in another year; the fringed gentian, set by Bryant in frayed and barren fields, frosty and solitary, usually follows the cardinal flower, in late September.

Come into the garden. The wind blows sharply from the north, where the snow still lies, and the clouds hang low, yet it is May-day, and a catbird is singing in the arbour. It is a much-trodden path in a long-discovered country, but each one discovers anew when he first sees it for himself. The golden touch, the guinea-stamp of Nature, is the dandelion in the grass border; flattened close to the sward, the wind passes over it, but bends and twists the masses of paler daffodils. The honeysuckles show pinched yellow leaves; the shrubs are bare, only the Forsythia is budded.

With what green intensity the pines are thrown into relief by the surrounding barrenness! In the top of one, a pair of crows are building, stealing forward and back with the distrust that is born of their small natures. Below, in a sheltered nook, patches of hardy violets are blooming: the little white violets that our grandmothers cherished, the odorous dark purple of the English garden-alleys, and the pansy-like variety from the

29

Russian Steppes, which, as they bloom, laugh at our frosty weather. In spots where the sun has rested, the cowslip shows its budded panicles, and a friendly hedge shelters a mat of yellow primroses, the flower of Tory dames. The same hedge harbours each season innumerable birds. Hark! that broken prelude is from the veery, or Wilson's thrush, as he darts into his shelter. Where the stone wall gathers every ray of heat, are rows of hyacinths, with ponderous trusses of bloom, rivalling in variety and richness of colouring any bulbous growth, and hordes of bees are thumping about them. If you wish to study colour, then stay awhile by these pansies, that jostle and overrun the borders like a good-natured crowd of boys. It is strange that we rarely see the most beautiful varieties in the markets or the flower shows. The trade florists grow them more for size and less for jewel-like markings. Here are solid colours, hues, veinings, tracings, and varied casts of expression, harlequin, sober, coquettish, as if continual hybridization had placed human intelligence in them . . . .

Go from the garden down through the lane to the meadow. What a burst of bird music greets you, solo, quartet, and chorus, led by the vivacious accentor, the golden-crowned thrush, with his crescendo of "Teacher—teacher—teacher!" This is the time and season to study the birds, while their plumage is fresh and typical, and they never sing so freely as in the first notes of their love song. The most puzzling part of the task is their modifications of plumage; for not only in many species are males and females totally different, but the male also changes his coat after the breeding season, and the nestlings wear a hybrid dress, half father, half mother. Does the gunner know that the bobolink, the jaunty Robert of Lincoln, whose glossy black coat, patched with white and buff, is so conspicuous in the lowlands when in May and June he rings out his delicious incoherent song, but who becomes silent in August and changed to a sober brown, is the reedbird that he slaughters? . . .

Look at the bank where the sun, peeping through, has touched the moss; there is saxifrage, and here are violet and white hepaticas, pushing through last year's leaves; lower down the wool-wrapped fronds of some large ferns are unfolding. The arbutus in the distant woods is on the wane, a fragrant memory. At the shady side of the spring are dog-tooth violets; and on the sunny side the watercourse is traced by clusters of marsh-marigolds, making a veritable golden trail. On a flat rock, almost hidden by layers of leaf mould, the polypody spreads its ferny carpet, and the little dicentra—or Dutchmen's breeches, as the children call it—huddles in clumps. The columbines are well budded, but Jack-in-the-pulpit has scarcely broken ground. On the top of the bank the dogwood stands unchanged, and the pinxter flower seems lifeless.

A brown bird, with reddish tail and buff, arrow-speckled breast, runs shyly through the underbrush, and perching on a low bush, begins a haunting, flute-like song. It is the hermit thrush. Its notes have been translated into syllables thus: "Oh speral, speral!

Oh holy, holy! Oh clear away, clear away; clear up, clear up!"—again and again he repeats and reiterates, until seeing us he slips into the bushes. . . .

Beyond the meadow a heavy belt of maples marks the coarse of the river; the gray, misty hue of winter has gone from their tops and they are flushed with red; the willows are yellow, and here and there show signs of leaf, but the white birches loom grim and chilling, with their tassels only expanded, and the anatomy of tree, bush, and brier is as clearly defined as in January. Bluebirds are very rare this spring; some chipmunks invaded their house last year, an intrusion which they sorely resented; but a number of warblers are flitting about, and feeding on young twigs or bark insects. The warblers, though insignificant singers, have the most varied and beautiful plumage; for a week, a flock of the black-throated green species has haunted a group of hemlocks, lighting the dark branches with glints of their gold and green feathers. The swallows are skimming over the meadow, and yesterday a belted kingfisher sat high in a dead maple by the river, with a flock of jays screaming and quarrelling near him. The snowbirds, buntings, nuthatches, and kinglets have passed to the north, as well as most of the owl tribe; but the little screech-owl remains to blink in the summer woods. Yonder black cloud, settling on the great chestnut, is an army of purple grackles, our crow blackbirds, and their glossy kin with the scarlet shoulders, whose cry is a shrill "Quank-a-ree," is the red-winged swamp blackbird.

Far down the meadow, where the grass is course and sedgy, and dry tussocks offer a shelter, the meadow lark is weaving its nest, working so deftly that its home is practically safe from human invaders. See him there, striding along in the full splendour of his plumage, dark brown above, with speckled sides, wings barred transversely, with brown, yellow breast, black throat-crescent, and yellow legs; while his mate is hardly less brilliant.

We must turn homeward now, for the birds are hurrying to shelter, the wind is rising, and the sound of the waves on the bar, two miles distant, is growing distinct and rhythmic. Big drops of rain are rustling in the dry beech leaves, the smoke of burning brush has enveloped the spring and shut off the meadow. The logs blazing on the hearth will give us a cheery welcome, for the mercury in the porch registers only ten degrees above freezing. Is it November? No, surely, but one of the twelve months has slept, and so wrought all this strange contradiction. This is the first of the Moon of Leaves, the May-day of Old England, and we have gathered violets and daffodils, and we have heard the hermit thrush singing in the lane:—

"The word of the sun to the sky,
The word of the wind to the sea,
The word of the moon to the night,
What may it be?"

31

MARY AUSTIN
(1868–1934)

*Mary Austin, a prolific writer of stories, poems, plays, and essays, was great-
ly influenced by the California high desert between the Sierra Nevada and
Death Valley, where she lived as a young woman after moving from Illinois.
The open spaces of this desert land and its native people inspired her collection of essays,* The Land of Little Rain *(1903), and the short stories in* Lost
Borders *(1909). The first chapter of* The Land of Little Rain *is one of
Austin's finest descriptions of the desert world. She is enchanted with this
mysterious land, full of risks and rewards; it is here she finds the source of
her spiritual strength.*

From *The Land of Little Rain*

EAST AWAY FROM THE SIERRAS, south from
Panamint and Amargosa, east and south many an uncounted mile, is the Country of
Lost Borders.

Ute, Paiute, Mojave, and Shoshone inhabit its frontiers, and as far into the heart of
it as a man dare go. Not the law, but the land sets the limit. Desert is the name it wears
upon the maps, but the Indian's is the better word. Desert is a loose term to indicate
land that supports no man; whether the land can be bitted and broken to that purpose
is not proven. Void of life it never is, however dry the air and villainous the soil.

This is the nature of that country. There are hills, rounded, blunt, burned,
squeezed up out of chaos, chrome and vermilion painted, aspiring to the snowline.
Between the hills lie high level-looking plains full of intolerable sun glare, or narrow
valleys drowned in a blue haze. The hill surface is streaked with ash drift and black,
unweathered lava flows. After rains water accumulates in the hollows of small closed
valleys, and, evaporating, leaves hard dry levels of pure desertness that get the local
name of dry lakes. Where the mountains are steep and the rains heavy, the pool is never
quite dry, but dark and bitter, rimmed about with the efflorescence of alkaline deposits.
A thin crust of it lies along the marsh over the vegetating area, which has neither beauty
nor freshness. In the broad wastes open to the wind the sand drifts in hummocks about
the stubby shrubs, and between them the soil shows saline traces. The sculpture of the

33

hills here is more wind than water work, though the quick storms do sometimes scar them past many a year's redeeming. In all the Western desert edges there are essays in miniature at the famed, terrible Grand Cañon, to which, if you keep on long enough in this country, you will come at last.

Since this is a hill country one expects to find springs, but not to depend upon them; for when found they are often brackish and unwholesome, or maddening, slow dribbles in a thirsty soil. Here you find the hot sink of Death Valley, or high rolling districts where the air has always a tang of frost. Here are the long heavy winds and breathless calms on the tilted mesas where dust devils dance, whirling up into a wide, pale sky. Here you have no rain when all the earth cries for it, or quick downpours called cloudbursts for violence. A land of lost rivers, with little in it to love; yet a land that once visited must be come back to inevitably. If it were not so there would be little told of it.

This is the country of three seasons. From June on to November it lies hot, still, and unbearable, sick with violent unrelieving storms; then on until April, chill, quiescent, drinking its scant rain and scanter snows; from April to the hot season again, blossoming, radiant, and seductive. These months are only approximate; later or earlier the rain-laden wind may drift up the water gate of the Colorado from the Gulf, and the land sets its seasons by the rain.

The desert floras shame us with their cheerful adaptations to the seasonal limitations. Their whole duty is to flower and fruit, and they do it hardly, or with tropical luxuriance, as the rain admits. It is recorded in the report of the Death Valley expedition that after a year of abundant rains, on the Colorado desert was found a specimen of Amaranthus ten feet high. A year later the same species in the same place matured in the drought at four inches. One hopes the land may breed like qualities in her human offspring, not tritely to "try," but to do. Seldom does the desert herb attain the full stature of the type. Extreme aridity and extreme altitude have the same dwarfing effect, so that we find in the high Sierras and in Death Valley related species in miniature that reach a comely growth in mean temperatures. Very fertile are the desert plants in expedients to prevent evaporation, turning their foliage edgewise toward the sun, growing silky hairs, exuding viscid gum. The wind, which has a long sweep, harries and helps them. It rolls up dunes about the stocky stems, encompassing and protective, and above the dunes, which may be, as with the mesquite, three times as high as a man, the blossoming twigs flourish and bear fruit.

There are many areas in the desert where drinkable water lies within a few feet of the surface, indicated by the mesquite and the bunch grass (*Sporobolus airoides*). It is this nearness of unimagined help that makes the tragedy of desert deaths. It is related that the final breakdown of that hapless party that gave Death Valley its forbidding name occurred in a locality where shallow wells would have saved them. But how were they to know that? Properly equipped it is possible to go safely across that ghastly sink, yet every year it takes its toll of death, and yet men find there sun-dried mummies, of whom no trace or recollection is preserved. To underestimate one's thirst, to pass a given landmark to the right or left, to find a dry spring where one looked for running water—there is no help for any of these things.

Along springs and sunken watercourses one is surprised to find such water-loving plants as grow widely in moist ground, but the true desert breeds its own kind, each in its particular habitat. The angle of the slope, the frontage of a hill, the structure of the soil determines the plant. South-looking hills are nearly bare, and the lower tree-line higher here by a thousand feet. cañons running east and west will have one wall naked and one clothed. Around dry lakes and marshes the herbage preserves a set and orderly arrangement. Most species have well-defined areas of growth, the best index the voiceless land can give the traveler of his whereabouts.

If you have any doubt about it, know that the desert begins with the creosote. This immortal shrub spreads down into Death Valley and up to the lower timberline, odorous and medicinal as you might guess from the name, wandlike, with shining fretted foliage. Its vivid green is grateful to the eye in a wilderness of gray and greenish white shrubs. In the spring it exudes a resinous gum which the Indians of those parts know how to use with pulverized rock for cementing arrow points to shafts. Trust Indians not to miss any virtues of the plant world!

Nothing the desert produces expresses it better than the unhappy growth of the tree yuccas. Tormented, thin forests of it stalk drearily in the high mesas, particularly in that triangular slip that fans out eastward from the meeting of the Sierras and coastwise hills where the first swings across the southern end of the San Joaquin Valley. The yucca bristles with bayonet-pointed leaves, dull green, growing shaggy with age, tipped with panicles of fetid, greenish bloom. After death, which is slow, the ghostly hollow network of its woody skeleton, with hardly power to rot, makes the moonlight fearful. Before the yucca has come to flower, while yet its bloom is a creamy cone-shaped bud of the size of a small cabbage, full of sugary sap, the Indians twist it deftly out of its fence of daggers and roast it for their own delectation. So it is that in those parts where man inhabits one sees young plants of *Yucca arborensis* infrequently. Other yuccas, cacti, low herbs, a thousand sorts, one finds journeying east from the coastwise hills. There is neither poverty of soil nor species to account for the sparseness of desert growth, but simply that each plant requires more room. So much earth must be pre.mpted to extract so much moisture. The real struggle for existence, the real brain of the plant, is underground; above there is room for a rounded perfect growth. In Death Valley, reputed the very core of desolation, are nearly two hundred identified species.

Above the lower tree-line, which is also the snow-line, mapped out abruptly by the sun, one finds spreading growth of piñon, juniper, branched nearly to the ground, lilac and sage, and scattering white pines.

There is no special preponderance of self-fertilized or wind-fertilized plants, but everywhere the demand for and evidence of insect life. Now where there are seeds and insects there will be birds and small mammals and where these are, will come the slinking, sharp-toothed kind that prey on them. Go as far as you dare in the heart of a lonely land, you cannot go so far that life and death are not before you. Painted lizards slip in and out of rock crevices, and pant on the white hot sands. Birds, hummingbirds even, nest in the cactus scrub; woodpeckers befriend the demoniac yuccas; out of the stark, treeless waste rings the music of the night-singing mockingbird. If it be summer and the sun well down, there will be a burrowing owl to call. Strange, furry, tricksy things dart across the open places, or sit motionless in the conning towers of the creosote. The poet may have "named all the birds without a gun," but not the fairy-footed, ground-inhabiting, furtive, small folk of the rainless regions. They are too many and too swift; how many you would not believe without seeing the footprint tracings in the sand. They are nearly all night workers, finding the days too hot and white. In mid-desert where there are no cattle, there are no birds of carrion, but if you go far in that direction the chances are that you will find yourself shadowed by their tilted wings. Nothing so large as a man can move unspied upon in that country, and they know well how the land deals with strangers. There are hints to be had here of the way in which a land forces new habits on its dwellers. The quick increase of suns at the end of spring sometimes overtakes birds in their nesting and effects a reversal of the ordinary manner of incubation. It becomes necessary to keep eggs cool rather than warm. One hot, stifling spring in the Little Antelope I had occasion to pass and repass frequently the nest of a pair of meadowlarks, located unhappily in the shelter of a very slender weed. I never caught them sitting except near night, but at midday they stood, or drooped above it, half fainting with pitifully parted bills, between their treasure and the sun. Sometimes both of them together with wings spread and half lifted continued a spot of shade in a temperature that constrained me at last in a fellow feeling to spare them a bit of canvas for permanent shelter. There was a fence in that country shutting in a cattle range, and along its fifteen miles of posts one could be sure of finding a bird or two in every strip of shadow; sometimes the sparrow and the hawk, with wings trailed and beaks parted, drooping in the white truce of noon.

If one is inclined to wonder at first how so many dwellers came to be in the loneliest land that ever came out of God's hands, what they do there and why stay, one does not wonder so much after having lived there. None other than this long brown land lays such a hold on the affections. The rainbow hills, the tender bluish mists, the luminous radiance of the spring, have the lotus charm. They trick the sense of time, so that once inhabiting there you always mean to go away without quite realizing that you have not done it. Men who have lived there, miners and cattle-men, will tell you this, not so fluently, but emphatically, cursing the land and going back to it. For one thing there is the divinest, cleanest air to be breathed anywhere in God's world. Some day the world will understand that, and the little oases on the windy tops of hills will harbor for healing its ailing, house-weary broods. There is promise there of great wealth in ores and earths, which is no wealth by reason of being so far removed from water and workable conditions, but men are bewitched by it and tempted to try the impossible.

You should hear Salty Williams tell how he used to drive eighteen and twenty-mule teams from the borax marsh to Mojave, ninety miles, with the trail wagon full of water barrels. Hot days the mules would go so mad for drink that the clank of the water bucket set them into an uproar of hideous, maimed noises, and a tangle of harness chains, while Salty would sit on the high seat with the sun glare heavy in his eyes, dealing out curses of pacification in a level, uninterested voice until the clamor fell off from sheer exhaustion. There was a line of shallow graves along that road; they used to count on dropping a man or two of every new gang of coolies brought out in the hot season. But when he lost his swamper, smitten without warning at the noon halt, Salty quit his job; he said it was "too durn hot." The swamper he buried by the way with stones upon him to keep the coyotes from digging him up, and seven years later I read the penciled lines on the pine headboard, still bright and unweathered.

But before that, driving up on the Mojave stage, I met Salty again crossing Indian Wells, his face from the high seat, tanned and ruddy as a harvest moon, looming through the golden dust above his eighteen mules. The land had called him.

The palpable sense of mystery in the desert air breeds fables, chiefly of lost treasure. Somewhere within its stark borders, if one believes report, is a hill strewn with nuggets; one seamed with virgin silver; an old clayey water-bed where Indians scooped up earth to make cooking pots and shaped them reeking with grains of pure gold. Old miners drifting about the desert edges, weathered into the semblance of the tawny hills, will tell you tales like these convincingly. After a little sojourn in that land you will believe them on their own account. It is a question whether it is not better to be bitten by the little horned snake of the desert that goes sidewise and strikes without coiling, than by the tradition of a lost mine.

And yet—and yet—is it not perhaps to satisfy expectation that one falls into the tragic key in writing of desertness? The more you wish of it the more you get, and in the mean time lose much of pleasantness. In that country which begins at the foot of the east slope of the Sierras and spreads out by less and less lofty hill ranges toward the Great Basin, it is possible to live with great zest, to have red blood and delicate joys, to pass and repass about one's daily performance an area that would make an Atlantic seaboard State, and that with no peril, and, according to our way of thought, no partic-ular difficulty. At any rate, it was not of whose waters, if any drink, they can no more see fact as naked fact, but all radiant with the color of romance. I, who must have drunk of it in my twice seven years' wanderings, am assured that it is worth while.

For all the toll the desert takes of a man it gives compensations, deep breaths, deep sleep, and the communion of the stars. It comes upon one with new force in the pauses of the night that the Chaldeans were a desert-bred people. It is hard to escape the sense of mastery as the stars move in the wide clear heavens to risings and settings unob-scured. They look large and near and palpitant; as if they moved on some stately service not needful to declare. Wheeling to their stations in the sky, they make the poor world-fret of no account. Of no account you who lie out there watching, nor the lean coyote that stands off in the scrub from you and howls and howls.

Marjorie Kinnan Rawlings
(1896–1953)

🌳

In 1928, Marjorie Kinnan Rawlings left behind a journalism career in Rochester, New York, and moved to Cross Creek, in the backwoods of north-central Florida. Here she farmed a small orange grove and continued to write, discovering in this unfamiliar place a compelling subject for her Pulitzer Prize–winning novel The Yearling *(1938), her memoir* Cross Creek *(1942), and other literary works.*

In "Hyacinth Drift," from Cross Creek, *Rawlings describes a boat trip on the St. John's River, which she and her friend Dessie embark upon against others' better judgment, for the river was notorious for its false channels and areas of wilderness. This river journey revives her spirits; and , when they get lost in the labyrinthian marshland, she learns the secret of navigating by paying attention to the signals of wind, water, and floating hyacinths. Like Isabella Bird, Rawlings discovers her ability to survive in wilderness; it is a discovery that brings "tremendous exhilaration."*

"Hyacinth Drift"

WAS PREPARED FOR MARSH. It was startling to discover that there was in sight literally nothing else. Far to the west, almost out of sight to the east, in a dark line like cloud banks was the distant swamp that edged this fluid prairie. We may have taken the wrong channel for a mile or so, for we never saw the sugar-berry tree; nothing but river grass, brittle and gold, interspersed, where the ground was highest, with butter-yellow flowers like tansy. By standing up in the boat I could see the rest of the universe. And the universe was yellow marsh, with a pitiless blue infinity over it, and we were lost at the bottom.

At five o'clock in the afternoon the river dissolved without warning into a two-mile spread of flat confusion. A mile of open water lay ahead of us, neither lake nor river nor slough. We advanced into the center. When we looked over our shoulders, the marsh had closed in over the channel by which we had come. We were in a labyrinth. The stretch of open water was merely the fluid heart of a maze. Channels extended out of it in a hundred directions—some shallow, obviously no outlets; others as broad as the stream we had left behind us, and tempting. We tried four. Each widened in a deceptive sweep. A circling of the shore-line showed there was no channel. Each time we returned to the one spot we could again identify—a point of marsh thrust into the water like a swimming moccasin.

Dess said, "That map and compass don't amount to much."

That was my fault. I was totally unable to follow the chart. I found later, too late for comfort, that my stupidity was not entirely to blame, for, after the long drought, half the channels charted no longer existed. The sun had become a prodigious red disc dropping into a distant slough. Blue herons flew over us to their night's quarters. Somewhere the river must continue neatly out of this desolation. We came back once more to the point of land. It was a foot or two out of water and a few square yards of the black muck were comparatively dry. We beached the rowboat and made camp.

There was no dry wood. We carried a bag of fat pine splinters but it occurred to me desperately that I would save them. I laid out a cold supper while Dess set up our two camp cots side by side on the open ground. As the sun slid under the marsh to the west, the full moon surged out of it to the east. The marsh was silver and the water was steel, with ridges of rippled ebony where ducks swam in the twilight. Mosquitoes sifted against us like a drift of needles. We were exhausted. We propped our mosquito bar over the cots on crossed oars, for there was no bush, no tree, from which to hang it.

We did not undress, but climbed under the blankets. Three people had had a hand in loading our cots and the wooden end-pieces were missing. The canvas lay limp instead of taut, and our feet hung over one end and our heads over the other, so that we were disposed like corpses on inadequate stretchers. The crossed oars slid slowly to the muck, the mosquito bar fluttered down and mosquitoes were about us in a swarm. Dess reached under her cot for her light rifle, propped it between us, and balanced the mosquito bar accurately on the end of its barrel.

"You can get more good out of a .22 rifle than any other kind of gun," she informed me earnestly.

I lay on my back in a torment of weariness, but there was no rest. I had never lain in so naked a place, bared so flatly to the sky. The moon swung high over us and there was no sleeping for the brightness. Toward morning dewdrops collected over the net-ting as though the moonlight had crystallized. I fell asleep under a diamond curtain and wakened with warm full sunlight on my face. Cranes and herons were wading the shore near me and Dess was in the rowboat a few hundred yards away, casting for bass.

Marsh and water glittered iridescent in the sun. The tropical March air was fresh and wind-washed. I was suddenly excited. I made campfire with fatwood splinters and cooked bacon and toast and coffee. Their fragrance eddied across the water and I saw

Dess lift her nose and put down her rod and reel. She too was excited.

"Young un," she called, "where's the channel?"

I pointed to the northeast and she nodded vehemently. It had come to both of us like a revelation that the water hyacinths were drifting faintly faster in that direction. From that instant we were never very long lost. Forever after, where the river sprawled in confusion, we might shut off the motor and study the floating hyacinths until we caught, in one direction, a swifter pulsing, as though we put our hands close and closer to the river's heart. It was very simple. Like all simple facts, it was necessary to discover it for oneself.

We had, in a moment, the feel of the river; a wisdom for its vagaries. When the current took us away that morning, we gave ourselves over to it. There was a tremendous exhilaration, an abandoning of fear. The new channel was the correct one, as we knew it should be. The river integrated itself again. The flat golden banks closed in on both sides of us, securing a snug safety. The strangeness of flowing water was gone, for it was all there was of living. . . .

MAY WYNNE LAMB
(1899–1975)

🌳

*May Wynne's decision to leave Kansas for Alaska in 1916 was considered an
odd choice for a single woman, but she was determined to live and work in
the Far North frontier. In the fall of 1916, she was employed as a government school teacher in a small Eskimo village on the Kuskokwim River in
southeastern Alaska; she lived there until the spring of 1919 when, after the
death of her husband, Frank Lamb, she went back to the United States.
Eventually she returned to Alaska to teach for another ten years. Her book,*
Life in Alaska: The Reminiscences of a Kansas Woman, *1914–1916
(1988), contributes to nature writing one of the few women settler's accounts
of life in the Alaskan wilderness. In this essay on the Kuskokwim River, a
waterway used then and now as a major source of travel, Lamb describes
the river's beauty and strength and shares her challenging experiences while
living along its shores.*

"The Kuskokwim River"

TOURISTS WHO VISIT ALASKA seldom travel
far enough west to see the beauties and magnificence of the Kuskokwim River. It is the
second largest river in Alaska, with its headquarters in the many unexplored regions of
the majestic Alaskan range. All the small, rushing, leaping streams unite in power to
provide a water basin of 50,000 square miles, and it affords 800 miles of navigation for
various kinds of watercraft. Oceangoing vessels navigate to Bethel, river steamers churn
the waters to McGrath, and graduated sizes of canoes and kayaks sail on the narrow,
shallow streams that are little more than babbling brooks.

The waters of the South, East, and North Forks together with the Takotna River
unite and combine to form the Kuskokwim proper. Here it gains in momentum and
power, mile by mile, as it is fed by the melting snow and ice, flowing through the many
unseen canyons to the great ocean. The Swift, the Stony, the Hoholitna, Crooked
Creek, and Tuluksak, with untold and unnamed sloughs, flow from all points of the
compass to help swell its magnitude. The mouth of the river, where it enters into the
Bering Sea, is a great source of worry to most navigators. The river channel is forever

changing. The mud flats spread out in low water as far as the eye can see. Sailors travel on half-tides. The low tides are too shallow and the high tides might leave them stranded on mudflats as the water reaches low ebb.

This awe-inspiring river has little recorded history since it is so isolated and inaccessible. It is practically unknown, compared with the much-written-about river Jordan, so inextricably interwoven with human life. Its history and its people are just coming to the front; in fact, many outside of Alaska have never heard of the word "Kuskokwim," meaning "cough river," "Kus" (cough) "kwim" (river).

This fast-moving stream sparkles on its way, animated and endowed with a fighting spirit; it twists and turns, whirls and leaps, burrows and squirms, both sides seeking madly to reach a goal. It has never been dammed or spanned; it stops for no umpire. It just keeps moving along as we do in life, intent on winning.

The Kuskokwim River not only gives pleasure and beauty, but bloodcurdling tales are told of its treachery and devouring terror. Dog teams and driver have plunged headlong through the ice to a watery, unknown grave; skaters at a gay and merry party have rushed heedlessly into unexpected air holes and been hopelessly lost under the ice; men in heavy trucks have crashed into the cold, deep water, tragically pinioned with no human means of escape; boats have been carried swiftly downward with all lost in the river's might and power.

The freeze-up was interesting, but it was quite different from what my geography led me to believe. The old river never waited until we were ready; year in and year out it had a task to perform. We might be caught far from home or with the boat held in its icy fangs. When nature set the time, it began blanketing itself with a lusty layer of ice, sometimes thinner and sometimes thicker, as the universe demanded. It made its own hibernal covering in much the same fashion as we would piece together a crazy quilt. The myriads of blocks of various shapes and sizes of one glistening color were so firmly integrated that only through the mighty power of old Sol could they be torn asunder.

A swift stream with whirlpools and powerful currents does not usually freeze over in just one night like a calm and tranquil lake; to begin with, the mighty Kuskokwim starts its refrigeration along the edges and then each day and night reaches out into the stream. When the action of the strong current breaks the ice loose from its moorings, it then floats downward toward the sea, joining to other broken parts. This process continues until the entire mass is consolidated and the river is firmly tucked in from bank to bank with its winter wrap. The days covered in this operation depend on the state of the weather and how quickly it acts to accomplish this enormous task. The ice now freezes thicker and deeper until it is safe for travelers—a seasonal highway that lasts for at least six months.

There is no temporizing with the weather either in the fall or spring; when the snow and ice in the many tributaries begin to melt, the water in the main river rises. This inundation lifts the ice, breaking the shore clasps loose from their anchor and leaving the whole mass free to follow the current. In its destructive and devouring momentum the ice is jammed and crushed into smaller pieces, producing a terrific thunderlike noise as it fights its way ruthlessly onward to the sea. In its mighty and mad force it works like an excavator, digging up the spruce and willow trees, shaving and gouging into the banks along the way, ever changing the bed of the river.

As the ice drifted by in a glamorous, lively parade, our imaginations pictured all kinds of sights on this fast-moving body. We fancied seeing men and their dog teams, cabins, animal life, and property of all kinds caught in the dangerous, monstrous, turbulent flow of ice and water; but our field glasses soon allayed our fears and put our minds at rest. It was only debris collected along the way.

The ice jammed our station, causing extreme high water for one day, and as a result we had a jolly good time sailing around the village in boats while it lasted. The government house and the church were the only spots high enough to escape the rip-roaring deluge. A boat was anchored at each door for emergency. During this time, we were packed with refugees for the night almost as tight as in our camp on the portage. Huge cakes of ice floated through the main street, and when the water suddenly dropped, these mammoth icebergs were left at our front doors to melt—a refrigeration that lasted for several days.

The Kuskokwim, a mellifluous name, flows through a very rich country, rich in various kinds of minerals, in many kinds of fish, in animal life, in grass and flowers, rich in beauty, a wonderful playland to those who love nature and the great God-given out-of-doors.

RACHEL CARSON
(1907–1964)

🌳

Rachel Carson, a marine biologist who worked for the U.S. Fish and Wildlife Service until 1952, became well known after she published Silent Spring *(1962), in which she documented pesticide's destructive influence on the environment. Her book led to a federal investigation and stricter regulations on pesticide use. But Carson also educated her readers about the significance of the living ocean in her first three books:* Under the Sea-Wind *(1941);* The Sea Around Us *(1950), which won the National Book Award for nonfiction in 1951 and the John Burroughs Medal for nature writing in 1952; and* The Edge of the Sea *(1955). Her work is a turning point in the history of women's nature writing because she combines scientific knowledge with descriptive, lyrical writing that appeals to a wide audience. In "Marginal World," Carson observes the tiny lives that exist at "the edge of the sea" and muses on "that intricate fabric of life by which one creature is linked with another, and each with its own surroundings."*

"The Marginal World"

THE EDGE OF THE SEA is a strange and beautiful place. All through the long history of Earth it has been an area of unrest where waves have broken heavily against the land, where the tides have pressed forward over the continents, receded, and then returned. For no two successive days is the shore line precisely the same. Not only do the tides advance and retreat in their eternal rhythms, but the level of the sea itself is never at rest. It rises or falls as the glaciers melt or grow, as the floor of the deep ocean basins shifts under its increasing load of sediments, or as the earth's crust along the continental margins warps up or down in adjustment to strain and tension. Today a little more land may belong to the sea, tomorrow a little less. Always the edge of the sea remains an elusive and indefinable boundary.

The shore has a dual nature, changing with the swing of the tides, belonging now to the land, now to the sea. On the ebb tide it knows the harsh extremes of the land world, being exposed to heat and cold, to wind, to rain and drying sun. On the flood tide it is a water world, returning briefly to the relative stability of the open sea.

Only the most hardy and adaptable can survive in a region so mutable, yet the area between the tide lines is crowded with plants and animals. In this difficult world of the shore, life displays its enormous toughness and vitality by occupying almost every conceivable niche. Visibly, it carpets the intertidal rocks; or half hidden, it descends into fissures and crevices, or hides under boulders, or lurks in the wet gloom of sea caves. Invisibly, where the casual observer would say there is no life, it lies deep in the sand, in burrows and tubes and passageways. It tunnels into solid rock and bores into peat and clay. It encrusts weeds or drifting spars or the hard, chitinous shell of a lobster. It exists minutely, as the film of bacteria that spreads over a rock surface or a wharf piling; as spheres of protozoa, small as pinpricks, sparkling at the surface of the sea; and as Lilliputian beings swimming through dark pools that lie between the grains of sand.

The shore is an ancient world, for as long as there has been an earth and sea there has been this place of the meeting of land and water. Yet it is a world that keeps alive the sense of continuing creation and of the relentless drive of life. Each time that I enter it, I gain some new awareness of its beauty and its deeper meanings, sensing that intricate fabric of life by which one creature is linked with another, and each with its surroundings.

In my thoughts of the shore, one place stands apart for its revelation of exquisite beauty. It is a pool hidden within a cave that one can visit only rarely and briefly when the lowest of the year's low tides fall below it, and perhaps from that very fact it acquires some of its special beauty. Choosing such a tide, I hoped for a glimpse of the pool. The ebb was to fall early in the morning. I knew that if the wind held from the northwest and no interfering swell ran in from a distant storm the level of the sea should drop below the entrance to the pool. There had been sudden ominous showers in the night, with rain like handfuls of gravel flung on the roof. When I looked out into the early morning the sky was full of a gray dawn light but the sun had not yet risen. Water and air were pallid. Across the bay the moon was a luminous disc in the western sky, suspended above the dim line of distant shore—the full August moon, drawing the tide to the low, low levels of the threshold of the alien sea world. As I watched, a gull flew by, above the spruces. Its breast was rosy with the light of the unrisen sun. The day was, after all, to be fair.

Later, as I stood above the tide near the entrance to the pool, the promise of that rosy light was sustained. From the base of the steep wall of rock on which I stood, a moss-covered ledge jutted seaward into deep water. In the surge at the rim of the ledge the dark fronds of oarweeds swayed, smooth and gleaming as leather. The projecting ledge was the path to the small hidden cave and its pool. Occasionally a swell, stronger than the rest, rolled smoothly over the rim and broke in foam against the cliff. But the intervals between such swells were long enough to admit me to the ledge and long enough for a glimpse of that fairy pool, so seldom and so briefly exposed.

And so I knelt on the wet carpet of sea moss and looked back into the dark cavern that held the pool in a shallow basin. The floor of the cave was only a few inches below the roof, and a mirror had been created in which all that grew on the ceiling was reflected in the still water below.

Under water that was clear as glass the pool was carpeted with green sponge. Gray patches of sea squirts glistened on the ceiling and colonies of soft coral were a pale apricot color. In the moment when I looked into the cave a little elfin starfish hung down, suspended by the merest thread, perhaps by only a single tube foot. It reached down to touch its own reflection, so perfectly delineated that there might have been, not one starfish, but two. The beauty of the reflected images and of the limpid pool itself was the poignant beauty of things that are ephemeral, existing only until the sea should return to fill the little cave.

Whenever I go down into this magical zone of the low water of the spring tides, I look for the most delicately beautiful of all the shore's inhabitants—flowers that are not plant but animal, blooming on the threshold of the deeper sea. In that fairy cave I was not disappointed. Hanging from its roof were the pendent flowers of the hydroid Tubularia, pale pink, fringed and delicate as the wind flower. Here were creatures so exquisitely fashioned that they seemed unreal, their beauty too fragile to exist in a world of crushing force. Yet every detail was functionally useful, every stalk and hydranth and petal-like tentacle fashioned for dealing with the realities of existence. I knew that they were merely waiting, in that moment of the tide's ebbing, for the return of the sea. Then in the rush of water, in the surge of surf and the pressure of the incoming tide, the delicate flower heads would stir with life. They would sway on their slender stalks, and their long tentacles would sweep the returning water, finding in it all that they needed for life.

And so in that enchanted place on the threshold of the sea the realities that possessed my mind were far from those of the land world I had left an hour before. In a different way the same sense of remoteness and of a world apart came to me in a twilight hour on a great beach on the coast of Georgia. I had come down after sunset and walked far out over sands that lay wet and gleaming, to the very edge of the retreating sea. Looking back across that immense flat, crossed by winding, water-filled gullies and here and there holding shallow pools left by the tide, I was filled with awareness that this intertidal area, although abandoned briefly and rhythmically by the sea, is always reclaimed by the rising tide. There at the edge of low water the beach with its reminders of the land seemed far away. The only sounds were those of the wind and the sea and the birds. There was one sound of wind moving over water, and another of water sliding over the sand and tumbling down the faces of its own wave forms. The flats were astir with birds, and the voice of the willet rang insistently. One of them stood at the edge of the water and gave its loud, urgent cry; an answer came from far up the beach and the two birds flew to join each other.

The flats took on a mysterious quality as dusk approached and the last evening light was reflected from the scattered pools and creeks. Then birds became only dark shadows, with no color discernible. Sanderlings scurried across the beach like little ghosts, and here and there the darker forms of the willets stood out. Often I could come very close to them before they would start up in alarm—the sanderlings running, the willets flying up, crying. Black skimmers flew along the ocean's edge silhouetted against the dull, metallic gleam, or they went flitting above the sand like large, dimly seen moths. Sometimes they "skimmed" the winding creeks of tidal water, where little spreading surface ripples marked the presence of small fish.

The shore at night is a different world, in which the very darkness that hides the distractions of daylight brings into sharper focus the elemental realities. Once, exploring the night beach, I surprised a small ghost crab in the searching beam of my torch. He was lying in a pit he had dug just above the surf, as though watching the sea and waiting. The blackness of the night possessed water, air, and beach. It was the darkness of an older world, before Man. There was no sound but the all-enveloping, primeval sounds of wind blowing over water and sand, and of waves crashing on the beach. There was no other visible life—just one small crab near the sea. I have seen hundreds of ghost crabs in other settings, but suddenly I was filled with the odd sensation that for the first time I knew the creature in its own world—that I understood, as never before, the essence of its being. In that moment time was suspended; the world to which I belonged did not exist and I might have been an onlooker from outer space. The little crab alone with the sea became a symbol that stood for life itself—for the delicate, destructible, yet incredibly vital force that somehow holds its place amid the harsh realities of the inorganic world.

The sense of creation comes with memories of a southern coast, where the sea and the mangroves, working together, are building a wilderness of thousands of small islands off the southwestern coast of Florida, separated from each other by a tortuous pattern of bays, lagoons, and narrow waterways. I remember a winter day when the sky was blue and drenched with sunlight; though there was no wind one was conscious of flowing air like cold clear crystal. I had landed on the surf-washed tip of one of those islands, and then worked my way around to the sheltered bay side. There I found the tide far out, exposing the broad mud flat of a cove bordered by the mangroves with their twisted branches, their glossy leaves, and their long prop roots reaching down, grasping and holding the mud, building the land out a little more, then again a little more.

The mud flats were strewn with the shells of that small, exquisitely colored mollusk, the rose tellin, looking like scattered petals of pink roses. There must have been a colony nearby, living buried just under the surface of the mud. At first the only creature visible was a small heron in gray and rusty plumage—a reddish egret that waded across the flat with the stealthy, hesitant movements of its kind. But other land creatures had been there, for a line of fresh tracks wound in and out among the mangrove roots, marking the path of a raccoon feeding on the oysters that gripped the supporting roots with projections from their shells. Soon I found the tracks of a shore bird, probably a sanderling, and followed them a little; then they turned toward the water and were lost, for the tide had erased them and made them as though they had never been.

Looking out over the cove I felt a strong sense of the inter-changeability of land and sea in this marginal world of the shore, and of the links between the life of the two. There was also an awareness of the past and of the continuing flow of time, obliterating much that had gone before, as the sea had that morning washed away the tracks of the bird.

The sequence and meaning of the drift of time were quietly summarized in the existence of hundreds of small snails—the mangrove periwinkles—browsing on the branches and roots of the trees. Once their ancestors had been sea dwellers, bound to the salt waters by every tie of their life processes. Little by little over the thousands and millions of years the ties had been broken, the snails had adjusted themselves to life out of water, and now today they were living many feet above the tide to which they only occasionally returned. And perhaps, who could say how many ages hence, there would be in their descendants not even this gesture of remembrance for the sea.

The spiral shells of other snails—those quite minute—left winding tracks on the mud as they moved about in search of food. They were horn shells, and when I saw them I had a nostalgic moment when I wished I might see what Audubon saw, a century and more ago. For such little horn shells were the food of the flamingo, once so numerous on this coast, and when I half closed my eyes I could almost imagine a flock of these magnificent flame birds feeding in that cove, filling it with their color. It was a mere yesterday in the life of the earth that they were there; in nature, time and space are relative matters, perhaps most truly perceived subjectively in occasional flashes of insight, sparked by such a magical hour and place.

There is a common thread that links these scenes and memories—the spectacle of life in all its varied manifestations as it has appeared, evolved, and sometimes died out. Underlying the beauty of the spectacle there is meaning and significance. It is the elusiveness of that meaning that haunts us, that sends us again and again into the natural world where the key to the riddle is hidden. It sends us back to the edge of the sea, where the drama of life played its first scene on earth and perhaps even its prelude; where the forces of evolution are at work today, as they have been since the appearance of what we know as life; and where the spectacle of living creatures faced by the cosmic realities of their world is crystal clear.

HELEN HOOVER
(1910–1984)

In 1954, Helen Hoover and her husband Adrian (Ade) left their jobs in Chicago and moved to the "edge of 593,000 acres" in the hilly, rocky land near the Minnesota Superior National Forest. Their life inspired Helen Hoover to write a series of books, including The Long-Shadowed Forest *(1963), a record of their early years learning to live in the wilderness. Hoover, who supported herself by writing, uses a straightforward style that enhances her serious approach to learning from the land. This essay from "King Weather" demonstrates how she and the animals around her cabin benefit from each other as they prepare for the isolated Minnesota winters during the final days of autumn.*

"King Weather"

AUTUMN BEGINS HERE in September, heralded not by flaring banners of color, but by the "fall sog." The sky is overcast; the air is chilly and windless; foggy ghosts, coiling downhill to drown themselves in the lake, eerily seem to pass through unresisting tree boles; drizzle brings damp that would make a frog rheumatic. Ade lights our first fire and its smoke falls wearily to the ground, joining with the dampness to add a smell of sodden burning to the dispiriting atmosphere. The exodus of summer people begins.

The wild things are in a fever of prewinter activity. I dump the feathers of a defunct pillow into a box in the woodshed and add a few newspapers for the convenience of nest refurbishers.

A squirrel investigates, then pulls and scratches and yanks mightily until she has detached a quarter-page of newsprint. She grasps its edge in her mouth and tries to push it ahead of her, but it traps her hurrying hind feet. She and the paper do a forward somersault off the woodshed floor onto the ground. She picks herself up, chattering anxiously, and examines her tail, which seems to have been twisted in the fall. Tail all right, she turns again to the paper, now somewhat crumpled. A wild skirmish ensues, in which the paper seems to take on a life of its own. Gradually it is torn and wadded until the squirrel discovers that she can cram it into her mouth and, with caution, hop across the yard.

At the foot of a black spruce she pats the paper into a tighter ball, squeaking and chirp-ing the while, before she begins the seventy-foot climb up the rough bark. The paper escapes from her teeth when she is a third of the way up, and down they come, the paper to sail off into some maple brush and the squirrel to land flat and sprawled on the duff. She sits up, paws across her chest, and, stamping her hind feet, complains vigorously about such undeserved harassment. That over, she goes after the paper, wads it up again, and this time makes it to the bough that bears her nest. She looks fearfully down at me as I walk toward the tree to watch, but deciding, perhaps, that I am not a climbing crea-ture, she carefully pats and crushes and pushes the paper into place.

Wondering how she knows that newspaper is fine insulation, I start for the cabin, but stop as a chipmunk, cheeks bulging with corn and mouth full of old-pillow feath-ers, skids to a stop in front of me. I stand perfectly still as she looks from one foot to the other and up, up, up to the top of my head. Reassured, she jumps between the feet of the colossus and scampers to the stone pile that protects her burrow entrance.

The chippy reminds me that I must send out the order for our own winter groceries before the freight stops its summer-only delivery. From the door, Ade is watching the squirrel as she begins a second assault on the obstreperous newspaper. "I guess it's time to seal up the roof," he says. He gets a ladder, and I dig the grocery catalog out of my file.

Then a chilling wind clears the day. The deciduous leaves, their work done, spiral down. Frost turns the fern fronds to buff and blackens summer flowers. Showers of pale-brown pine needles trim the roof and weave intricate carpets on the paths, hang like fringe on the fences around the abandoned garden, and throw a network over the dwindling squash plants. Pine cones thump on the roof and fall to the ground. Cedar leaves the color of iron ore thicken the layer of duff. When the wind's task is complet-ed, the trees are clear green again. The seeds of a bull thistle float high on fall air whose tang creeps into the blood, to stir and ripple and emerge in an effervescence of delight.

There are many wings over the water as the flocks of ducks gather and the young ones practice take-offs and landings. Often one, not quite strong enough, runs on the surface, trying to lift with its brothers. Perhaps it will fly south with them, perhaps not. If it cannot migrate, it will die. Nature does not coddle the weak.

The ducks disappear, the geese fly over, and the green hills across the lake wear crests and brocades of gold. Ade and I, if our work allows leisure time, cross the huge rocks that guard our shore and take a boat ride. As we paddle out from the skid, we admire our mountain ash, its leaves a weaving of pale-yellow daggers against which its scarlet berries hang over the water. The gray jays are snatching the fruits, dropping many of them. The spilled berries bleed on the stones or disappear in little splashing fountains. There is movement under the water but the rippled surface is too deeply shadowed for us to see what lake dweller is feeding on such beautiful food.

The arc of the sun is shortening for winter and our south shore is in shadow. On the edge of the lake, maples flame scarlet and alders modestly display foliage of dusty rose. The smooth water is black-green, reflecting the autumn trees like searchlights turned down into the depths—a brightly colored inversion of the northern lights. Among the evergreens, the birches and aspens show pale green in sheltered spots, buttercup gold in the open, shining bronze where the big ones rise above young spruces, and rusty on the ridges where the leaves wait to fall in the wind.

The shadows of the past lie on the hills. Where glacial till alternates with ridges of rock, wide yellow swaths follow the soil from the water to the hilltops, and stunted cedars cling by twisted roots to crevices in the stone. Nearby stands of climax forest, grown through centuries and many cycles of grasses, shrubs, and various trees to full maturity. The stubby limbs of its black spruces, rising high above the aspens, are so thickly needled that the trees are top-heavy. Behind them, surviving white pines remember their fallen brothers. In the distance a saw-toothed ripple bears witness to an ancient folding of the earth. The nearer hills, where evergreens and red deciduous treetops mark the slopes with hieroglyphic designs, are veiled ever so lightly with blue, while those more distant grow fainter row on row in a purple haze, the worn-down roots of the mountains.

We leave behind us the last of the lodges and cabins, and idle beneath granite bluffs, splotched with the maroon and green of lichens. In a little bay we come upon a beaver house. One beaver swims slowly across the water, its head leaving a rippled streak behind. We think we are unseen but, with a splash and a scattering of drops, its flat tail slaps the water in warning. We marvel at the swift, water-skimming flight of a pair of late golden-eyes. We paddle carefully through shallows where the jagged black teeth of the earth snarl up at us through the water. We stretch our legs on a secluded beach, where a stream pours out a green tunnel.

The sun is low in the northwest. Ade starts the outboard and turns homeward over water that is flat and milky-blue in the evening calm. I watch the waves curling away from the boat in moving sculpture to collapse in a flurry of bubbles at the sides of our wake. At first the waves are blue with silver arabesques flowing over them, their bubbles clear and rainbow glinting, their scattered drops white like pearls or touched by shadow into spheres of blackness. Our trail upon the water lies behind us, gradually turning from turquoise to green. The slanting light is darkening from white to saffron to bronze, and details of the shore stand out in amber-traced clarity. The waves are green now, their patterns and droplets glowing like melted copper. The light begins to fade rapidly, and the waves are violet meshed with restless black.

In the west, a cloudbank is forming, rayed from its flaming edges by the hidden sun. A wind is rising and there is a chill in the air. Far ahead of us whitecaps flash across the ultramarine water like leaping fish. Ade opens the throttle and we race the squall home.

As we haul the boat to safety on its cedar-log skid, the wind reaches across the lake, beating the rolling water into foam-edged combers. Thunderheads are thrusting into a third of the sky and their voices rumble in the distance as the first lightning streaks over the forest. We run to the log cabin, ducking our heads against puffs of dusty, twig-laden air.

Unmindful of the weather, the tame squirrels are gathered in the yard for an evening snack after their long day of cone harvesting. We hand them graham crackers, while chickadees and woodpeckers, blue and gray jays, pick suet from feeders and snatch corn and crackers from the ground.

Suddenly the storm, cloaked in premature darkness, roars toward us through the trees and we and the wild things take cover. Inside, by the mellow light of oil lamps, we listen to the strange voices in the wind, to the crash and thud of waves breaking on the rocks. We hear the crack-crack-crack-snap of a big tree falling nearby. Ade blows out all the lamps except those near us, which we can extinguish quickly. If a tree should strike the house, we do not want fire to add horror to confusion. Torrents drum on the roof and pour from the eaves; beyond the black windows, the forest appears and reappears in lightning-white flares; thunder blasts and reverberates between hills and clouds.

Then it is over. The sky clears from the west. Water drops glimmer softly along the eaves as the twilight fades into night. It is time to light all the lamps, draw the curtains against the big dark, eat, and reopen the books we laid down the night before....

MARY LEISTER

(1917–)

Mary Leister's nature essays were first published in the Baltimore Sun, *and then collected in* Wildlings *(1976) and* Seasons at Heron Pond *(1981). In* Wildlings *she describes her "territory," a square mile of Howard County, Maryland—its woodlands, marshes, ponds, and fields—where she has lived for many years. As she roams with her dog Kela, Leister discovers the unusual in the natural world; she is adept at looking behind leaves, under rocks, and inside trees to observe what most people easily overlook. Her keen observation skills are evident in these two essays, which relate how sudden changes in the weather lead to some surprising discoveries.*

"Hot as a Flicker's Nest"

ALONG THE WESTERN SLOPES of the Allegheny mountains, in years past, when any countryman spoke of a grossly overheated area, whether heated by stove or sun, he used the ultimate simile to describe it: "It's hot as a flicker's nest in there!"

How hot, I wondered every time I heard the expression, can a flicker's nest be? It became a childhood ambition to put my hand into a flicker's nest to learn for myself just how excessive the heat was in there. But the few flicker nests I ever discovered were high up in great old trees whose lowest limbs were well beyond my reach, and, though I did some energetic climbing in nearby trees, I never quite managed to get close enough to a nest to test its temperature.

Thus, on a certain April morning when I caught the glint of golden underwings from a mated pair of flickers, I watched with more than casual interest. They were hunting a nesting site among the trees on either side of the shallow creek in my neighbor's marsh. Perhaps, after all these years, a nest might be located low enough so that, with thermometer in hand, I could find out exactly how hot "as hot as a flicker's nest" is.

The two birds investigated every knot hole and hollow and tapped exploratory bills along a hundred interesting limbs and trunks without finding exactly what they wanted. The mustachioed male did cut a few whopping chips from the wildcherry tree on the high bank, making the black bark and the light inner wood fly in all directions, but the female flew at him with scolding cries until he left off his sculpting and followed her on an inspection tour of the sassafras grove on the top of the hill.

From the sassafras grove they flew to the oak and hickory woods that stretched across the lower end of the small valley, searched it for a day and a half, then worked their way back up the marsh until they reached an ancient willow just below the pond in the middle of the valley. And here they stopped. Only eight feet up on the rough-barked trunk they immediately chipped out a circle nearly three inches across and chiseled a hole three or four inches deep straight back from the opening.

Only eight feet up! I could scarcely wait for their nesting to begin. But, after that enterprising opening, the birds suddenly became indolent. They flew about the marsh and the pond on no errands whatever, or sat, tail-braced, on the trunks of neighboring trees and filled the April air with their wickering. Then they found an ant hill in the fence corner across the marsh and spent long hours sprawling about on the great crumbly mound, occasionally tucking black-and-red ants under their wings, and constantly thrusting their sticky tongues into the ant hill openings to collect mouthfuls of plump, lemon-flavored ants. And nearly a week went by before the nesting hole was completed.

But when it was done it was a beautifully carved-out cylinder in the heart of the willow trunk. A dark cell nearly eighteen inches deep and more than six inches across, it had a round doorway already polished by their comings and goings. Inside, a few wood chips and a sprinkling of sawdust on the floor made it comfortable for the brooding flickers and their eventual babies. The grasses at the foot of the willow were thickly littered with untidy scatterings of large-chiseled wood chips and rough-powdered sawdust.

Finally, quite early on an April morning, when the countryside was shrouded in fog and a fine drizzle fell through it, the female flicker entered her new willow-wood home and settled herself to produce her first egg. The male pecked around at the bark of the nearby mulberry trees, eating a few insect eggs or new-hatched grubs to pass the time. Every so often he flew over to perch in the willow tree and to talk softly to his mate hidden away inside the trunk.

It was well past the middle of morning and the mist still fell softly through the gray fog. Suddenly, the valley was filled with vivid streaks of light flashing up, flashing down, from a blazing, quivering nucleus of light high up in the fog, while the air tightened, then rocked apart with intense explosive sound. The willow tree split from top to bottom, through the middle of its giant trunk, right through the middle of the new flicker nest. The scorched limbs and charred branches flew through the air, scattering for hundreds of feet along the creek bank and out into the marsh.

The male disappeared never to be seen again, nor any trace of him found. His mate still sat on the gray ashes of the wood chips on the bottom of one-half of her cylindrical nest, her feathers vanished, her brick-red flesh baked dry to her bones.

In the earlier hours of that morning I stood near the willow watching the course of the flicker's nesting, but at the moment of violence I was nearly half a mile away, just opening the back door of my home. I felt the strange sensation which I can only call a "tightening" of the air, saw the wild leapings of light, was enveloped in the unbelievable force of the explosive sound.

And all that day and all that night the fog and the fine drizzle continued, but there was not another flash of light, not another burst of sound, not even a quiet rumble. It is possible, I suppose, that, just as in a winter snow a charge of electricity is sometimes generated to be discharged in a surprising flash of lightning and resultant thunder, so, possibly, a charge was built up in the constant-drizzle-through-the-fog to be discharged dramatically on that April day.

One wonders, of course, why in that particular spot? Why that particular willow tree? Did the hollow within that tree, heated by that little flicker body, have anything to do with the electrical attraction? Whatever the reason, one thing I know beyond doubt—for one catastrophic instant that was surely the hottest flicker's nest ever to be known or imagined.

* * * * *

"Of Winter Fogs and Hoarfrost"

The fogs of January rarely steal in on little cat feet. They roll in like the tide, and they trail whole seas behind them. These are seas that billow thick and white and all-concealing over harbor and city and the countryside beyond; silent seas that muffle other sounds; unstoppable seas that slow the commerce of man—until the fog moves on.

And January fogs are in no hurry to move. They thin or vanish in the middle of the day, like the tide gone out, and return with the setting of the sun for a week or more at a time. January fogs can hang on horizons all the day and roll in slowly and inexorably when darkness falls, or they can suddenly and dramatically engulf the daylight world.

On a January morning, several years ago, following a series of such fogs that came soon after a deep-drifting snow, the sun rose clear and bright against a cloudless sky. Stark black tree-trunks forested the woodlands, diamonds and sapphires danced from the snowdrifts, and the clefts in the hills were deep in blue shadows.

The thermometer read fifteen degrees, and Kela and I, starting our morning walk, crunched through frozen snow that covered grasses and stones and all the little game trails in forests and fields.

We visited the den of a red fox in a high outcropping and were crossing the ravine below it when a haze began to rise from the bulge of the hill ahead of us. We had scarcely taken two more steps before it became a wall of fog, thick and white and cottony. I stopped in amazement. Kela stopped, too; not, I think, because I stopped, but to watch it for herself. In moments its stretched the entire length of the field and increased in height from probably one foot, when I first noticed it, to eight feet or ten. It materialized out of nothingness, a fog suddenly there where it had not been an instant before.

And suddenly there was no longer a wall in front of us. We were, ourselves, engulfed. We stood in a bowl, white-bottomed, white-walled, white-lidded, and there was no up or down or sideways.

Imagine a fog like this on a western prairie! I tried to frighten myself with the thought of being lost in a vast, unmarked space. I ignored the clear path of our footprints in the snow, which, however meandering, would lead to our own front door, and mentally tried my trackless wilderness. Fifty yards below us was a fence which, if followed in one direction, would lead to a neighbor's barn, and, if followed in the other, would lead to our own woods; and if we followed the far edge of the woods we'd come to our own backyard. No matter which way we walked from that spot, I realized, we'd come to a neighbor's buildings, or our own woods, or the county road. We were safe.

I suspect we would have been anyway, for although we walked through an opaque whiteness that smelled like steam and turned to prickly frost in our nostrils, Kela went directly to the one spot in the pasture fence where we can get through easily, and led unhesitatingly across the marsh to the creek, up the creek to the pond which we could see only in small, misty portions; and then, swiftly, up the ravine that splits the hill pasture.

Just as we topped the hill the enveloping fog rose slowly and visibly to hang a few feet above my head. I could look down the hill to the marsh and out across the hilltop to the countryside beyond. Everything lay clear and distant under a ten-foot ceiling, and everything wore a furry coat it had not worn before the fog appeared.

Every twig, every branch, every brown leaf was rimed with spicular hoar frost. The brown stalks of goldenrod and the gray stalks of thistle that rose above the snow were coated in crystal. But not fully coated, I noticed when I examined them. Only their northern and eastern surfaces were frosted, and the frost was a thick-clustered fur of fine, long needles, crystal white. And every icy needle pointed to the northeast.

All through the fields, the woods, the clearing, I checked this orientation. On dogwood and hickory, oak and cedar, walnut and maple, on honeysuckle, aster, goldenrod and sedge, every furry spike pointed steadfastly to the northeast. There were needle rays, too, lying flat on the packed snow of our footprints, each long ray thick in the middle and tapering finely at the ends.

I phoned a meteorologist friend ten miles away. He assured me I had taken leave of my senses. "There is no fog!" he said. "There is out here," I answered, but he denied it. "I know it takes just the right set of conditions to bring all this about," I told him, "but it *has* happened. We have a fifty-foot ceiling now and the whole world out here is dressed in frost needles. Every one of those needles is at least three-eighths of an inch long, and every one of those needles is pointing toward the northeast." My friend's denials ceased and he said, very softly, into the mouthpiece, "They'd *have* to point northeast. There's a gentle airflow from the southwest."

Just as suddenly as it had come, the fog disappeared. The sun shone, and the hoar-frost vanished as though it had never been. Again, the long tree trunks stood black in the woodlands, diamonds and sapphires danced from the snowdrifts, and blue shadows marked the deep clefts in the hills.

MAXINE KUMIN
(1925–)

🌳

From a hillside farm in Warner, New Hampshire, writer and farm owner Maxine Kumin meditates on land and animals' influence on her writing life and sense of place. Although most widely known as a poet—having won the Pulitzer Prize in 1973 for Up Country: Poems of New England *and serving as the Consultant in Poetry to the Library of Congress for 1981–1982—Kumin has also written novels, short stories, essays, and children's books. Her journal selections from the collection* In Deep: Country Essays *(1987) give us an imtimate look at the daily activities of farm life during that transitional time when people and animals wait impatiently for winter to turn to spring.*

"Journal—Late Winter–Spring 1978"

13 February 1978—Today, in the dying butternut tree that holds up the clothesline from which depend various suets and the main sunflower-seed feeder, an owl. Peterson's indicates it is a barred owl, not an unusual bird in these surroundings. He arrived, like a poem, unannounced. He squatted on the branch, puffed to an almost perfect round-ness against the cold. His gray and brown and buff markings imitate the landscape of tree branch and caterpillar nest tatters against the snow. I could not, as the cliché has it, believe my eyes at first, and tried to make him into some recognizable artifact of nature—a clump of windblown leaves, for example. Like the notes for a poem, he would not go away but merely swelled there passively all through breakfast.

The squirrels did not show themselves, wisely. The chickadees are fearless, or at least know they have nothing to fear. The blue jays likewise. I note that our narrow-faced, downside-traveling nuthatches were absent all day.

14 February—The owl is a Cheshire cat of an owl, noiselessly appearing, disappearing, flapping off soundlessly on immense wings, returning, higher up than before. He swivels his head almost 360 degrees, like a Japanese puppet-balloon held aloft on a stick. The face is infinitely old, infinitely wise, very catlike. When perched, no wings or claws are evident, lending him even more mystery than is warranted. Like the finished poem, he makes it all seem easy. Not since last winter's wild turkeys, not since last summer's swallow nestling sideshow on the front porch stringers, has there been better indoor viewing.

15 February—This resident owl of ours, I muse on the third day of his tenure in the butternut, resembles nothing birdlike. Most of all he looks like a baseball pitcher in a tight spot, winding up, swiveling to check the runners at first and second, then . . . the balk. The old owls of my poems were of the furtive sort, night hooters. Whenever I did catch a daytime glimpse of them, they were in a hurry to get under cover and they seemed ragged, weary, diminished by a hard night's work. This one is larger than life-size. He has assumed the stature of a godhead in the birdfeeding zone, though today he and the squirrel eyed each other and nothing happened. Perhaps the owl is full of his nightly mice? I noticed that the squirrel took care, while cleaning up the spilled sun-flower husks, not to turn his back on the owl. Although only a small red squirrel, per-haps he is too large to tempt even an enlarged owl.

20 February—The filly these cold mornings canters in place in her stall. Too excited to tuck into her morning hay, she wants desperately to be let out, to run off some of that adolescent exuberance. Some days it is impossible to get a halter on her before her morning run. Today I unleashed her early and stood in the barn doorway to enjoy the aesthetics of her romp. The young horse is so improbably gracefully made; the body itself has not yet filled out, the legs are still disproportionately long. That extraordinary high tail carriage, the whole plume of it arched over her back, and the floating suspend-ed gait she displays at the trot, are inherited from her pure Arabian sire. It takes quite a lot of racing, dodging, cavorting, and bucking to get the morning kinks out. She can come to a dead stop from, say, thirty miles an hour. She can attain that speed in, say, three strides. What she does is harsher than ballet, and less controlled, something like dribbling down a basketball court, feinting, shooting, wheeling, back to the other end, and so on. The exultation I feel as I watch her move so freely and with such euphoria is a kind of glorying in effortlessness, no matter how much muscle is involved. She moves the way a poem ought to move, once it's crafted.

24 February—Putting in the spiles I lean on the brace and bit, having to use all my weight to keep the metal spiral angling upward into the tough tree. How astonishing, after the hole is bored, that the sap glistens, quivers, begins to run freely. To think that I have never seen or done this before! I am as captivated as the city child finding out where milk comes from.

We have cobbled a Rube Goldberg sort of contraption for boiling the sap down: an ancient kitchen sink for an evaporator, leftover bits of corrugated metal roofing to enclose the fire, a rack and grill from a long-abandoned fireplace gadget that was designed to throw heat back into the room but failed to do so to an appreciable degree, and two rusty pieces of stovepipe, one with a damper. Plus piles of trash wood, pine, primarily, which gives off too much pitch to be safe to burn indoors.

1 March—Although it is still too cold for any appreciable melt, one tree—we note that it's on higher ground that the others and thicker, too—is really running. The sap freezes almost as much as it drips, forming a great colorless cake of possibility. John Burroughs, quoted by the Nearings in their maple syrup text, says: "The first run, like first love, is always the best, always the fullest, always the sweetest."

How much still is dormant! And how the spirit yammers at the spirit hole, howling for spring to inch in. Now the horses are shedding, a gradual, indifferent sort of daily loss. Both Jack and the Boomer have grown an extra outer coat of coarse, short white guard hairs. These fly off in the slightest wind or are rubbed off, with grunts of horse pleasure, as they roll in the sun on the snow. Truffle, a mare of more refinement and considerable bloodlines, pure bay, has no such tough outer layer. Now that she is eight months pregnant she rolls only on one side, gets up, lies down anew to roll onto the other. Three months still to go. The foal will come at the end of May, in the full throat of spring.

Today I started half a dozen flats for the garden, of French celery and big-leaved basil, broccoli and cauliflower, and, optimistically because they always die of indoor wilt before it is time to set them out, some miniature hybrid tomatoes. Our bedroom is now crowded with trays hogging the available south light of two windows. Step stools, their step sides facing the windows, make ideal shelves on top of the counter that runs along the south wall. The secret is that I put some aged manure in the bottom of each tray. I hope it is sufficiently ancient so that it won't, at room temperature, begin to reek.

7 March—The chickadees have changed their tune and are now singing their mating song. Those same beggars who perched on my arm in January while I was filling their feeder now stay away most of the morning. They are citizens of independent means.

11 March—Everything is softening. The change, when it came, was direct, happened overnight. In spite of longing, reaching for it for weeks, we were still overtaken. The sap is running, a delightful chorus of plink-plinks in the sugarbush.* The horses are shedding apace. They itch enough to roll every morning now, all the guard hairs a drift of fuzz in the air, free to nesting birds for the taking.

---

*In 1982, we converted to tubing.

The other night we did the barn chores together and stood a while enjoying Jack enjoying his hay. Wise old campaigner, he totes it by the mouthful to his water bucket and dunks as he crunches, not unlike the way our forebears crunched sugar lumps as they sucked up their tea. Soon the surface of Jack's water is a yellowish froth from the hayseeds. Alternately he sucks and chews, a moist rhythm.

13 March—The morning one is convinced it is spring there is a rising, manic elation for having outlasted the winter, for having come through, in Conrad's phrase, unscathed, with no bones broken. Last evening at feeding time two crows went across the paddock cawing in midair, and I felt goosebumps rising at the nape of my neck. That crows know when to return! That ice will melt, snow cover shrink, days lengthen! Nothing is to be taken for granted after a winter of below-zero mornings, ice frozen in all the water buckets, the horses' nostrils rimmed with ice. After north winds that scour and cleanse and punish. After nights so cold the house clapboards crack and whine. Now the bad times ebb. The split wood lasted, we shall even have a cord or so to spare, as a hedge toward next winter. We calculated correctly on the hay, we congratulate ourselves on its quality, none of it dusty or moldy, enough of it so we can be generous. And Truffle now swelling and swelling, retreating more into herself, less sociable, more self-protective. In a few more weeks we will separate her, almost nine months of her eleven-month gestation now over.

29 April—This last week of April, all those little lurchings toward spring have landed us smack in the middle of the season. Pine siskins, crossbills, evening grosbeaks are back. Robins, redwing blackbirds, and cowbirds are back. The indefatigable barn swallows are back, swooping and diving hard for the first insects. My flats of tomatoes are now hardening out on the porch; they look healthy enough to flourish in the earth in a few more weeks. The broccoli and cauliflower have been transplanted into the cold frame where they seem to be standing still, sulking. All my winter dill died while I was in Utah. But the parsley we kept as a house pet right through from October is bushy and strong and as of today is back out of doors. Early peas are going in today.

Some few blackflies are abroad, particularly in the pasture when the wind dies. Just enough to remind us of the incursion to come. Just enough to make me want to press on with planting before they peak.

15 May—Who can keep a journal past the first week of May? All in a one-day seizure, cattails, fiddlehead ferns, and nettles up for the picking. Nettle soup for supper. Three days later, marsh marigolds, which my neighbor Henry calls, as the British do, cowslips.

The exquisite tedium of preparing the garden, plowing in last winter's manure, adding lime, destoning, smoothing with the patience if not the dexterity of frosting a cake. If you live with an engineer, you respectfully measure and line up your rows, keep a garden plan on graph paper and do your homework. Did I add half a day's labor to refurbish the fence of chicken wire, eight inches of which is buried to foil woodchucks, moles, voles, and mice? Meanwhile the air has filled with blackflies. Some days, if we are to speak out of doors, we inhale them. Some days, like this one, a blessed breeze holds them hovering at bay.

May means grass, manna to the horses after a winter of hay. They set about browsing with ferocious intensity. The tonic of spring juices creates a considerable amount of whinnying and squealing and racing, ruckus of the variety called horsing around. Everyone has lost his/her winter coat. The filly positively shines, like a simonized Jaguar. Truffle is ponderous and grave, she walks as though her feet hurt and perhaps they do, as she totes that heavy unborn foal from day to day.

Fulsome bird life. The feeder overcrowded with rose-breasted grosbeaks, purple finches, and half a dozen goldfinches queued up on the clothesline awaiting an opportunity. The swallows are nesting. They made their usual slapdash repairs to the nests over the brick terrace and once the eggs are hatched will shriek alarm and dive-bomb me if I dare to exit through that door. My peas are up, tentatively. The onions seem off to a strong start.

The peepers were later this year than any year I can remember. They did not give voice until May 8 and only this week have they found their true range. Once they're in full swing, it is deafening to walk by the lower pond at sunset. It is the purest form of noise pollution.

ANN ZWINGER
(1925–)

🌳

*For the past twenty years, Ann Zwinger has been writing and illustrating
books on the western landscape, including* Beyond the Aspen Grove
(1970), Run, River, Run *(1975), which won the John Burroughs Medal,
and* Wind in the Rock *(1978). In* The Mysterious Lands *(1989), she
describes her exploration of the four great desert regions—the Chihuahuan,
the Sonoran, the Mojave, and Nevada's Great Basin—and intersperses
detailed botanical information with personal narrative. In the following
essay, Zwinger narrates her experience of camping alone in the Sonoran
Desert while on a volunteer assignment to count bighorn sheep. From her
careful observations of plants and animals and description of her own adaptation to the excessive desert temperatures, we gain a heightened appreciation for both the hazards and the pleasures of the Sonoran Desert.*

"Of White-Winged Doves and Desert Bighorns"

CABEZA PRIETA means "dark head" in
Spanish, and the peak that inspired that name blocks the horizon in front of us, a pyra-
mid of pearly-tan schist draped with a hangman's hood of black lava. It identifies the
Cabeza Prieta Mountains, a forbidding fault black mountain range rising from an endless, boundless desert beset with a dryness and heat that devour colors and horizons and
fade outlines until all that is left is shimmer.

This third week in June I enter the Cabeza Prieta National Wildlife Refuge with
Chuck Bowden and Bill Broyles, both of whom have a desert fixation. When someone
asks them why they go to the desert, they figure it's like J.P. Morgan's being asked how
much his yacht cost. Bill, who in his sensible life is an English teacher, drives this road
with an insane joy in the required high-clearance, four-wheel-drive vehicle. We enter
the Cabeza from the north, and it seems to me we have come thousands of miles from
refuge headquarters, where we have been briefed on bighorn sheep counting, driving
first on highways, then narrow roads, then dirt roads, and now this ridiculous track.

"Road" is a euphemism. When wet, it imbibes rear axles. When dry, it buries you
in sand for hours at a time. It has tracks with ruts that snap a wheel, high centered

enough to batter a crankcase to oblivion. Washboard is too complimentary a word. We're talking lurching, jolting, tilting, loose-rock or deep-sand, kidney-busting roads that just don't care whether you travel them or not. Ocotillos, rude toll takers, thrust their thorny hands into the open window with intent to rob. On this questionable road, not only does one eat dust, and smell an overloaded and overheated engine, but also has to endure the squeals of vegetation dragging its fingernails along the sides of the truck, thorny plants as ill-tempered as the road itself.

We have volunteered to take part in a formal yearly desert bighorn-sheep count that has been done here since 1961. In 1939 ninety bighorns were estimated to be on the refuge; today the number is approximately three hundred.

Desert bighorns roam the mountain range of the Cabeza in male and female bands (young rams are included in both) throughout most of the year, getting enough water and vegetation. They combine and come in to water holes only during the driest months of the year, May and June. The commingling announces the onset of the herd's breeding season, correlated to producing lambs at the most propitious time, a timing that varies in each desert bighorn herd according to the particular mountain-range climate in which it lives.

We bounce into the small east-west valley that holds the tank where I will be stationed. The valley is narrow, rising to a notch between two high granite ridges to the west. Without gentling bajadas, the mountains bolt out of the floor, rubbled and pitted, short and steep, boldly tilted, roughed out with a chisel but never worked down or refined.

Bill offloads three jerry cans of water, enough for my six days here, a folding chair, and a cot. He and Chuck will go on to their own stations twenty miles away. I heave my duffel down, eager for them to be gone, anxious to set up desert housekeeping, ready to begin these days of immaculate isolation. The truck disappears in a cloud of dust, and for a moment I just stand quietly, blissfully alone. Then I unfold my chair, set up the tripod, and mount and focus the spotting telescope on the far slope, where I hope the sheep will be, wire the thermometer at eye level, and survey my kingdom.

The blind is half-hidden beneath an ancient mesquite tree. Open in the rear and with a window facing the natural water pocket of the tank, it is made of four steel posts faced with saguaro ribs. The plywood roof has wallboard nailed underneath, and, in the space between, a heaping of mesquite twigs and pods hints at a wood-rat nest, a suspicion soon confirmed when the occupant itself sashays off to forage.

The tinaja itself is invisible from the blind. It is tucked to the right against a vertical wall, two hundred yards up the draw. Huge boulders flank it on the left; one, fifteen feet high, provides a provident perch for the several dozen birds that frequent it. Tomorrow I shall walk up to record its water level.

Promptly at 7:00 P.M. bats begin cruising the campsite, looping lower than I'm used to seeing bats fly, whishing right past my ear, winnowing the air for insects with great efficiency. After they leave, I get bitten. The light fades so gently that my eyes are adjusted to starlight by 9:30 P.M. when I go to bed. The air is a comfortable 86 degrees F. The quiet is soporific. An infinitesimal breeze feathers my ankles and face all night long, the gentlest whisper of air in a great friendliness of night. Gazing up through the lacy canopy of mesquite leaves, I try only to doze, unwilling to miss anything. I do not succeed.

In the midst of a sound sleep, a sudden gust of wind looses an avalanche of mesquite twigs and pods and I shoot awake. The moon fingerpaints the sky with clouds. The Milky Way forms a great handle to the basket of the earth in which I lie. It is deliciously cool, enough so to pull up my sleeping bag. When I awake again, a big old saguaro hoists the near-full moon on its shoulder. By 4:30 A.M., when sheep watchers are expected to be sentient and at their task, pearly-gray light seeps into the valley.

Mesquite pods litter my sleeping bag and shoes. My cup holds three like swizzle sticks. These mesquites have longer, slimmer fruits, smaller leaves and leaflets, and a larger number of leaflets than those in damper climes. Unlike other pea family pods, these do not split open but retain the seeds embedded in a hard covering, and an animal that eats one must eat pod and all. So important were they to the prehistoric Seri Indians who inhabited Sonora, Mexico, that they had names for eight different stages of fruit development. The Seris even sifted through wood-rat nests several months after harvest to recover the mesquite seeds; their high protein and carbohydrate content made them a significant addition to their diet. Other desert Indians, the Amargosa and Pinacate:o, developed a special gyratory crusher for grinding them. All I can say from experience is that the fruits are as hard as rocks, dry as bones, fall like lead weights, and truly do taste sweet. . . .

In the noon stillness, the heat presses down, lies as heavy as a mohair wool blanket on my head, on my shoulders. It's only 108 degrees; knowing it can get up to 130 degrees in these close canyons, I am thankful for small favors. The air around the rocks near the rock tank wavers with banners of heat. I feel stooped and bent with heat as I leave the shade of the blind to walk up to the tinaja. I need to record the tank's water level so I can see how much water evaporates during the week (it goes down 3 1/4 inches). Bursage leaves disintegrate as I brush by them. Where there is shallow groundwater, mesquite and big clumps of saltbush outline the wash, many of them festooned with vining milkweed, twined and twisted in great heaps like a giant-size helping of vermicelli. Seed pods load catclaw, how ripe the seeds are depending on where the bush is set. By the blind the seeds are still green and held tightly in the pod; lower, they are drying to a salmon color, and in the hollow at the foot of the draw, they are dark brown and shiny, rattling in the twisted pods.

Up the slope, a four-foot-high elephant tree has found a purchase in the rocky slope along the trail, leaves just perceptible, ready to unfold the moment it rains. The papery-barked trunks, fat for water storage, give off a familiar turpentine odor. Hollyleaf bur sage, endemic to the lower Sonoran, marches up the slope to the ridge crest. This bur sage retains its scalloped leaves for years, the oldest faded nearly pure white. Now nettlelike seed heads remain, blooming over for the year.

The granite surrounding the water tank is pale gray, crystalline, flecked with sparkling black mica and roughened with large quartz crystals. Like most tinajas here, it lies in the crease of a small stream channel. A silt-holding wall has been built above the pool, and some cementing at the lower end provides an apron where animals can safely approach the water. Higher water levels limn the rocky sides with gray lines, and an inch of vivid green algae circles the present pool. It swarms with bees, ravenous for water to replace the large amount they lose in flight. I hesitate a long minute, then make my measurement as quickly as possible because in recent years I've become allergic to bee stings.

Anaphylactic shock, due to bee or insect stings, is not common, but on a percentage basis, it kills more people than venomous snakebite does. While it would take over a hundred stings to affect a nonsensitized person, just one sting can cause anaphylactic shock within minutes in one who is sensitized. Mellitin, a basic protein composed of thirteen different amino acids, is the chief toxin. It affects the permeability of skin capillaries, instigates a drop in blood pressure followed by a swift rise, can cause severe asthma, damage nerves and muscle tissue. In fatalities, the allergic reaction to the sting causes a drop in blood pressure so massive that no oxygen gets to the heart or brain. With immediate medical help a necessity, and none within a hundred miles, I am exceedingly conservative.

On the way back to the blind, still thinking about venomous bites, I round a boulder and gasp: five feet in front of me, on a large flat rock, is a Gila monster, a fearsome-looking lizard because it's so big. The size of my forearm, its tail is massive and thick, a repository for fat and water. Vivid warning colors of black and light yellowish orange pattern its beaded skin. With only two venomous lizards in the whole wide world, I nearly have to fall over one of them.

After a Gila monster locks onto its victim with its jaws, it chews. While doing so, it injects venom from glands set just under the skin of the lower jaw. Each tooth has sharp flanges flanking the grooves through which the venom flows, making its virulent bite very painful. In small animals death comes from respiratory paralysis. Although the bite brings severe pain and swelling, quickly followed by nausea and weakness, it is not usually fatal to human beings.

Gila monsters generally hunt at night during hot weather and are out during the day only in cooler seasons. Their metabolism is so low that they need to eat infrequently, and then prefer the eggs of reptiles and birds and the young of small rodents. I cannot imagine why it is out at this time of day. I back off with more speed than grace and leave it to its meditation.

An innocent little four-inch zebra-tailed lizard, perhaps more tan-and-white than zebra-striped, scampers across the sand, its ringed tail curled up over its back like a pug dog. One of the fastest lizards around, it has a chevron pattern on its back and legs that blends in with the flickering shadows and becomes invisible when it skitters under an acacia. I watch it dully. By comparison, my legs feel made of lead....

The sheep do not come in until the second day, as if they were waiting to be sure their intruder was from a friendly planet. As I periodically scan the mountain slope with binoculars, it is some moments before I realize that the "rocks" are moving. I nearly tip over the spotting scope in my delight and eagerness to get it focused. The bighorns come downslope with a deliberate, measured tread, pausing occasionally to stand and look about or pull off an acacia twig. Either eight or nine gather at the tinaja, and they change places just often enough to make them exasperatingly difficult to count.

My first impression is of smallness and grace. Less than four feet high at the shoulder, they move easily over what I know to be a ruggedly steep and treacherous slope. With their smooth coats and long legs they bear little resemblance to domestic sheep, to which they are *not* related. The genus *Ovis* originated in Eurasia more than two and a half million years ago, migrated, as man did, across the Bering Land Bridge, and became isolated into different groups during glacial periods. Today desert bighorns inhabit the arid mountain ranges of the southwest deserts.

Although I observe no pushing or shoving, clearly there exists a hierarchy at the water tank. A large, mature ewe waters first, taking two-minute and then four-minute drafts, and then stands aside. She has shed most of her winter coat but a continuous remnant cloaks her shoulders like a shawl, making her easy to identify when she appears again. Bighorn shedding begins at the rump and moves forward. All the other sheep have less old pelage clinging, suggesting that this ewe may be an older animal. She is accompanied by two lambs with their mothers that never go down to drink. The ability of desert bighorns to go without water exceeds even that of the camel. Their extensive rumen complex—the first stomach of ruminant animals—holds and supplies enough water to support their needs. They produce a concentrated urine and to some extent resorb moisture from their feces. They can drink rapidly enough to get back into water balance within five minutes.

The next morning the large ewe again waters first, taking two long drinks before she leaves. Other sheep move in, young ewes and/or yearling rams—their size and horn shape are so close that I cannot differentiate at this distance. Mature rams are easy to identify, as the horns are much more developed and the four-year mark is usually a very prominent and readily visible groove on the horn, especially visible from the back. From that line one counts rings back toward the head for a fairly accurate age estimate, as each ring marks the cessation of growth for one year. The sheep remain at the tank, either drinking or standing around, for half an hour, and then slowly amble up the hill.

After they leave, a single large ram comes to drink. His horns have almost a full curl with the ends broomed off, leaving the tips worn and blunt (brooming results from rubbing the horns against rocks and dirt). The ram takes almost ten minutes to come down the hillside. After reading about their prowess in leaping rocks and sheer cliffs, covering ground with astonishing leaps and bounds, I am struck by his extreme deliberateness, which I take also to be a measure of his serenity. I dutifully record that he drinks for two minutes, then six, then two more minutes before mincing his way back up the hill.

Meanwhile the earlier crew reach the crest of the ridge to the east and disappear over the rim. The ram stops twenty feet or so below the top, where a ewe and her lamb lie hidden in a shadowy niche. He nuzzles the lamb, which tags along after him over the hill. The ewe remains, entering a deep overhang I have not noticed before, disappearing from view in the shadow.

I am inordinately pleased. I feel as if the sheep have honored me with their presence and I find myself smiling as I write up my observations.

Ursula K. Le Guin

(1929–)

The natural world and the use of myths to explore that world is an integral part of Ursula K. Le Guin's writing; this is particularly evident in her science fiction and fantasy writing, including The Earthsea Trilogy *(1977). Her essay, "A Very Warm Mountain," also considers the role of myth in the 1980 eruption of Mount St. Helens. At the time, Le Guin was recovering from surgery and had a window view of the volcano forty-five miles north of her home in Portland, Oregon. Her essay tracks the developments of the volcano's activities and the various ways in which people personalized the event in order to "reduce it to human scale." Le Guin's essay interprets the feminine imagery of the volcano from a unique perspective. Of Mount St. Helens, she writes, "...she is a woman. And not a mother but a sister."*

"A Very Warm Mountain"

AN ENORMOUS REGION extending from north-central Washington to northeastern California and including most of Oregon east of the Cascades is covered by basalt lava flows.... The unending cliffs of basalt along the Columbia River...74 volcanoes in the Portland area...A blanket of pumice that averages about 50 feet thick....

—Roadside Geology of Oregon
Alt and Hyndman, 1978

Everybody takes it personally. Some get mad. Damn stupid mountain went and dumped all that dirty gritty glassy gray ash that flies like flour and lies like cement all over their roofs, roads, and rhododendrons. Now they have to clean it up. And the scientists are a real big help, all they'll say is we don't know, we can't tell, she might dump another load of ash on you just when you've got it all cleaned up. It's an outrage.

Some take it ethically. She lay and watched her forests being cut and her elk being hunted and her lakes being fished and fouled and her ecology being tampered with and the smoky, snarling suburbs creeping closer to her skirts, until she saw it was time to teach the White Man's Children a lesson. And she did. In the process of the lesson, she blew her forests to matchsticks, fried her elk, boiled her fish, wrecked her ecosystem, and did very little damage to the cities: so that the lesson taught to the White Man's Children would seem, at best, equivocal.

But everybody takes it personally. We try to reduce it to human scale. To make a molehill out of the mountain.

Some got very anxious, especially during the dreary white weather that hung around the area after May 18 (the first great eruption, when she blew 1300 feet of her summit all over Washington, Idaho, and points east) and May 25 (the first considerable ashfall in the thickly populated Portland area west of the mountain). Farmers in Washington State who had the real fallout, six inches of ash smothering their crops, answered the reporters' questions with polite stoicism; but in town a lot of people were cross and dull and jumpy. Some erratic behavior, some really weird driving. "Everybody on my bus coming to work these days talks to everybody else, they never used to." "Everybody on my bus coming to work sits there like a stone instead of talking to each other like they used to." Some welcomed the mild sense of urgency and emergency as bringing people together in mutual support. Some—the old, the ill—were terrified beyond reassurance. Psychologists reported that psychotics had promptly incorporated the volcano into their private systems; some thought they were controlling her, and some thought she was controlling them. Businessmen, whom we know from the Dow Jones Reports to be an almost ethereally timid and emotional breed, read the scare stories in Eastern newspapers and cancelled all their conventions here; Portland hotels are having a long cool summer. A Chinese Cultural Attaché, evidently preferring earthquakes, wouldn't come farther north than San Francisco. But many natives were irrationally exhilarated, secretly, heartlessly welcoming every steam-blast and earth-tremor: Go it, mountain!

Everybody read in the newspapers everywhere that the May 18 eruption was "five hundred times greater than the bomb dropped on Hiroshima." Some reflected that we have bombs much more than five hundred times more powerful than the 1945 bombs. But these are never mentioned in the comparisons. Perhaps it would upset people in Moscow, Idaho or Missoula, Montana, who got a lot of volcanic ash dumped on them, and don't want to have to think, what if that stuff had been radioactive? It really isn't nice to talk about it, is it. I mean, what if something went off in New Jersey, say, and *was* radioactive—Oh, stop it. That volcano's way out west there somewhere anyhow.

Everybody takes it personally.

I had to go into hospital for some surgery in April, while the mountain was in her early phase—she jumped and rumbled, like the Uncles in *A Child's Christmas in Wales*, but she hadn't done anything spectacular. I was hoping she wouldn't perform while I couldn't watch. She obliged and held off for a month. On May 18 I was home, lying around with the cats, with a ringside view: bedroom and study look straight north about forty-five miles to the mountain.

I kept the radio tuned to a good country western station and listened to the reports as they came in, and wrote down some of the things they said. For the first couple of hours there was a lot of confusion and contradiction, but no panic, then or later. Late in the morning a man who had been about twenty miles from the blast described it: "Pumice-balls and mud-balls began falling for about a quarter of an hour, then the stuff got smaller, and by nine it was completely and totally black dark. You couldn't see ten feet in front of you!" He spoke with energy and admiration. Falling mud-balls, what next? The main West Coast artery, I-5, was soon closed because of the mud and wreckage rushing down the Toutle River towards the highway bridges. Walla Walla, 160 miles east, reported in to say their street lights had come on automatically at about ten in the morning. The Spokane-Seattle highway, far to the north, was closed, said an official expressionless voice, "on account of darkness."

At one-thirty that afternoon, I wrote:

It has been warm with a white high haze all morning, since six A.M., when I saw the top of the mountain floating dark against yellow-rose sunrise sky above the haze.

That was, of course, the last time I saw or will ever see that peak.

Now we can see the mountain from the base to near the summit. The mountain itself is whitish in the haze. All morning there has been this long, cobalt-bluish drift to the east from where the summit would be. And about ten o'clock there began to be visible clots, like cottage cheese curds, above the summit. Now the eruption cloud is visible from the summit of the mountain till obscured by a cloud layer at about twice the height of the mountain, i.e., 25-30,000 feet. The eruption cloud is very solid-looking, like sculptured marble, a beautiful blue in the deep relief of baroque curls, sworls, curled-cloud-shapes—darkening towards the top—a wonderful color. One is aware of motion, but (being shaky, and looking through shaky binoculars) I don't actually see the carven-blue-sworl-shapes move. Like the shadow on a sundial. It is enormous. *Forty-five miles away. It is so much bigger than the mountain itself. It is silent, from this distance. Enormous, silent. It looks not like anything earthy, from the earth, but it does not look like anything atmospheric, a natural cloud, either. The blue of it is storm-cloud blue but the shapes are far more delicate, complex, and immense than stormcloud shapes, and it has this solid look; a weightiness, like the capital of some unimaginable column—which in a way indeed it is, the pillar of fire being underground.*

At four in the afternoon a reporter said cautiously, "Earthquakes are being felt in the metropolitan area," to which I added, with feeling, "I'll say they are!" I had decided not to panic unless the cats did. Animals are supposed to know about earthquakes, aren't they? I don't know what our cats know; they lay asleep in various restful and decorative poses on the swaying floor and the jiggling bed, and paid no attention to anything except dinner time. I was not allowed to panic.

At four-thirty a meteorologist, explaining the height of that massive, storm-blue pillar of cloud, said charmingly, "You must understand that the mountain is very warm. Warm enough to lift the air over it to 75,000 feet."

And a reporter: "Heavy mud flow on Shoestring Glacier, with continuous lightning." I tried to imagine that scene. I went to the television, and there it was. The radio and television coverage, right through, was splendid. One forgets the joyful courage of reporters and cameramen when there is something worth reporting, a real Watergate, a real volcano.

On the 19th, I wrote down from the radio, "A helicopter picked the logger up while he was sitting on a log surrounded by a mud flow." This rescue was filmed and shown on television: the tiny figure crouching hopeless in the huge abomination of ash and mud. I don't know if this man was one of the loggers who later died in the Emanuel Hospital burn center, or if he survived. They were already beginning to talk about the "killer eruption," as if the mountain had murdered with intent. Taking it personally . . . Of course she killed. Or did they kill themselves? Old Harry who wouldn't leave his lodge and his whiskey and his eighteen cats at Spirit Lake, and quite right too, at eighty-three; and the young cameraman and the young geologist, both up there on the north side on the job of their lives; and the loggers who went back to work because logging was their living; and the tourists who thought a volcano is like Channel Six, if you don't like the show you turn it off, and took their RVs and their kids up past the road-blocks and the reasonable warnings and the weary county sheriffs sick of arguing: they were all there to keep the appointment. Who made the appointment?

A firefighter pilot that day said to the radio interviewer, "We do what the mountain says. It's not ready for us to go in."

On the 21st I wrote:

Last night a long, strange, glowing twilight; but no ash has yet fallen west of the mountain. Today, fine, gray, mild, dense Oregon rain. Yesterday afternoon we could see her vaguely through the glasses. Looking appallingly lessened—short, flat—That is painful. She was so beautiful. She hurled her beauty in dust clear to the Atlantic shore, she made sunsets and sunrises of it, she gave it to the western wind. I hope she erupts magma and begins to build herself again. But I guess she is still unbuilding. The Pres. of the U.S. came today to see her. I wonder if he thinks he is on her level. Of course he could destroy much more than she has destroyed if he took a mind to.

On June 4 I wrote:

Could see her through the glasses for the first time in two weeks or so. It's been dreary white weather with a couple of hours sun in the afternoons.— Not the new summit, yet; that's always in the roil of cloud/plume. But both her long lovely flanks. A good deal of new snow has fallen on her (while we had rain), and her SW face is white, black, and gray, much seamed, in unfamiliar patterns.
    "As changeless as the hills—"
    Part of the glory of it is being included in an event on the geologic scale. Being enlarged. "I shall lift up mine eyes unto the hills," yes: "whence cometh my help."

In all the Indian legends dug out by newspaper writers for the occasion, the mountain is female. Told in the Dick-and-Jane style considered appropriate for popular reportage of Indian myth, with all the syllables hyphenated, the stories seem even more naive and trivial than myths out of context generally do. But the theme of the mountain as woman—first ugly, then beautiful, but always a woman—is consistent. The mapmaking whites of course named the peak after a man, an Englishman who took his title, Baron St. Helens, from a town in the North Country: but the name is obstinately feminine. The Baron is forgotten, Helen remains. The whites who lived on and near the mountain called it The Lady. Called her The Lady. It seems impossible not to take her personally. In twenty years of living through a window from her I guess I have never really thought of her as "it."

    She made weather, like all single peaks. She put on hats of cloud, and took them off again, and tried a different shape, and sent them all skimming off across the sky. She wore veils: around the neck, across the breast: white, silver, silver-gray, gray-blue. Her taste was impeccable. She knew the weathers that became her, and how to wear the snow.

Dr. William Hamilton of Portland State University wrote a lovely piece for the college paper about "volcano anxiety," suggesting that the silver cone of St. Helens had been in human eyes a breast, and saying:

> *St. Helens' real damage to us is not . . . that we have witnessed a denial of the trustworthiness of God (such denials are our familiar friends). It is the perfection of the mother that has been spoiled, for part of her breast has been removed. Our metaphor has had a mastectomy.*
>
> *At some deep level, the eruption of Mt. St. Helens has become a new metaphor for the very opposite of stability—for that greatest of twentieth-century fears—cancer. Our uneasiness may well rest on more elusive levels than dirty windshields.*

This comes far closer to home than anything else I've read about the "meaning" of the eruption, and yet for me it doesn't work. Maybe it would work better for men. The trouble is, I never saw St. Helens as a breast. Some mountains, yes: Twin Peaks in San Francisco, of course, and other round, sweet California hills—breasts, bellies, eggs, anything maternal, bounteous, yielding. But St. Helens in my eyes was never part of a woman; she is a woman. And not a mother but a sister.

These emotional perceptions and responses sound quite foolish when written out in rational prose, but the fact is that, to me, the eruption was all mixed up with the women's movement. It may be silly but there it is; along the same lines, do you know any woman who wasn't rooting for Genuine Risk to take the Triple Crown? Part of my satisfaction and exultation at each eruption was unmistakably feminist solidarity. You men think you're the only ones can make a really nasty mess? You think you got all the firepower, and God's on your side? You think you run things? Watch this, gents. Watch the Lady act like a woman.

For that's what she did. The well-behaved, quiet, pretty, serene, domestic creature peaceably yielding herself to the uses of man all of sudden said NO. And she spat dirt and smoke and steam. She blackened half her face, in those first March days, like an angry brat. She fouled herself like a mad old harridan. She swore and belched and farted, threatened and shook and swelled, and then she spoke. They heard her voice two hundred miles away. Here I go, she said. I'm doing my thing now. Old Nobodaddy you better JUMP!

Her thing turns out to be more like childbirth than anything else, to my way of thinking. But not on our scale, not in our terms. Why should she speak in our terms or stoop to our scale? Why should she bear any birth that we can recognize? To us it is cataclysm and destruction and deformity. To her—well, for the language for it one must go to the scientists or to the poets. To the geologists. St. Helens is doing exactly what she "ought" to do—playing her part in the great pattern of events perceived by that noble discipline. Geology provides the only time-scale large enough to include the behavior of a volcano without deforming it. Geology, or poetry, which can see a mountain and a cloud as, after all, very similar phenomena. Shelley's cloud can speak for St. Helens:

> *I silently laugh*
> *At my own cenotaph . . .*
> *And arise, and unbuild it again.*

So many mornings waking I have seen her from the window before any other thing: dark against red daybreak, silvery in summer light, faint above river-valley fog. So many times I have watched her at evening, the faintest outline in mist, immense, remote, serene: the center, the central stone. A self across the air, a sister self, a stone. "The stone is at the center," I wrote in a poem about her years ago. But the poem is impertinent. All I can say is impertinent.

When I was writing the first draft of this essay in California, on July 23, she erupted again, sending her plume to 60,000 feet. Yesterday, August 7, as I was typing the words "the 'meaning' of the eruption," I checked out the study window and there it was, the towering blue cloud against the quiet northern sky—the fifth major eruption. How long may her labor be? A year, ten years, ten thousand? We cannot predict what she may or might or will do, now, or next, or for the rest of our lives, or ever. A threat: a terror: a fulfillment. This is what serenity is built on. This unmakes the metaphors. This is beyond us, and we must take it personally. This is the ground we walk on.

SUE HUBBELL
(1935–)

*A former librarian at Brown University, Sue Hubbell now keeps bees on a
farm in the Ozarks of Southern Missouri, where she has lived since 1973.
Her first book,* A Country Year: Living the Questions *(1986), narrates her
personal changes as a middle-aged woman living independently in rural
Missouri. Here, she discovers in the natural world an order and logic that
revives her sense of existence. These two essays reveal her sensitivity towards
even the tiniest lives that share the land with her, and she describes with
fine detail how their unexpected behavior enriches her life.*

"Spring"

ONE SPRING EVENING a couple of years ago,
I was sitting in the brown leather chair in the living room reading the newspaper and
minding my own business when I became aware that I was no longer alone.

Looking up, I discovered that the three big windows that run from floor to ceiling
were covered with frogs.

There were hundreds of them, inch-long frogs with delicate webbed feet whose fin-
gerlike toes ended in round pads that enabled them to cling to the smooth surface of
the glass. From their toe structure, size and light-colored bellies, I supposed them to be
spring peepers, *Hyla crucifer,* and went outside for a closer look. I had to be careful
where I put my feet, for the grass in front of the windows was thick with frogs, waiting
in patient ranks to move up to the lighted surface of the glass. Sure enough, each pink-
ish-brownish frog had a back criss-crossed with the dark markings that give the species
its scientific name. I had not known before that they were attracted to light.

I let my newspaper go and spent the evening watching them. They did not move
much beyond the top of the windows, but clung to the glass or the moldings, seemingly unable to decide what to do next. The following morning they were gone, and I have
never seen them at the windows since. It struck me as curious behavior.

These window climbers were silent; we usually are only aware of spring peepers at
winter's end—I first hear their shrill bell-like mating calls in February from the pond
up in the field. The males produce the calls by closing their mouths and nasal openings

and forcing air from their lungs over the vocal cords into their mouths, and then back over the vocal cords into the lungs again. This sound attracts the females to the pond, and when they enter the water the males embrace them, positioning their vents directly above those of the females. The females then lay their eggs, which the males fertilize with their milt.

It is a clubby thing, this frog mating, and the frogs are so many and their calls so shrill and intense that I like to walk up to the pond in the evenings and listen to the chorus, which, to a human, is both exhilarating and oddly disturbing at close range. One evening I walked there with a friend, and we sat by the edge of the pond for a long time. Conversation was inappropriate, but even if it had not it would have been impossible. The bell-like chorus completely surrounded us, filled us. It seemed to reverberate with the shrill insistence of hysteria, driving focused thought from our heads, forcing us not only to hear sound but to feel it.

Comparing notes as we walked back to my cabin, we were startled to discover that we had both wondered, independently, whether that was what it was like to go mad.

A slightly larger cousin of the spring peeper that belongs to the same genus, the gray tree frog, commonly lives in my beehives during the summer months. These frogs cling under the protective overhang of the hive cover, and as I pry up the lid, they hop calmly to the white inner cover and sit there placidly eying me.

They are a pleasing soft grayish-green, marked with darker moss-colored patches, and look like a bit of lichen-covered bark when they are on a tree. Having evolved this wonderfully successful protective coloration, the safest behavior for a gray tree frog in a tight spot is to stay still and pretend to be a piece of bark. Sitting on the white inner cover of the beehive, the frog's protective coloration serves him not at all, but of course he doesn't know that, and not having learned any value in conspicuously hopping away, he continues to sit there looking at me with what appears to be smug self-satisfaction and righteous spunk.

Last evening I was reading in bed and felt rather than heard a soft plop on the bed next to me. Peering over the top of my glasses, I saw a plump, proud gray tree frog inspecting me. We studied each other for quite a time, the gray tree frog seemingly at ease, until I picked him up, carried him out the back door and put him on the hickory tree there. But even in my cupped hands he moved very little, and after I put him on the tree he sat quietly, blending in beautifully with the bark. A serene frog.

The sills in my bedroom are rotten, so I supposed that he had found a hole to come through and wondered if he'd had friends. I looked under the bed and discovered three more gray tree frogs, possibly each one a frog prince. Nevertheless, I transferred them to the hickory.

There was something in the back of my mind from childhood Sunday-school class-es about a plague of frogs, so I took down my Bible and settled back in bed to search for it. I found the story in Exodus. It was one of those plagues that God sent to convince the Pharaoh to let the Jews leave Egypt.

And the Lord spake unto Moses, Go unto Pharaoh, and say unto him, Thus saith the Lord, Let my people go, that they may serve me.
And if thou refuse to let them go, behold, I will smite all thy borders with frogs:
And the river shall bring forth frogs abundantly, which shall go up and come into thine house, and into thy bedchamber, and upon thy bed . . .

This was exciting stuff; my evening had taken on a positively biblical quality. I was having a plague of frogs, and had obviously had another the evening that the spring peepers had crawled up the living-room windows. Actually, I enjoyed both plagues, but Pharaoh didn't. The writer of Exodus tells us that Pharaoh was so distressed by frogs in his bed that he called Moses and said,

Intreat the Lord, that he may take away the frogs from me, and from my people; and I will let the people go, that they may do sacrifice unto the Lord.

A fussy man, that Pharaoh, and one easily unnerved.

I once knew a pickerel frog, *Rana palustris,* frog of the marshes, who might have changed Pharaoh's mind. The pickerel frog was an appealing creature who lived in my barn one whole summer. He was handsome, grayish with dark, square blotches high-lighted with yellow on his legs. I found him in the barn one morning trying to escape the attentions of the cat and the dogs. At some point he had lost the foot from his right front leg, and although the stump was well healed, his hop was awkward and lopsided. I decided that he would be better off taking his chances with wild things, so I carried him out to the pond and left him under the protective bramble thicket that grows there. But the next day he was back in the barn, having hopped the length of a football field to get there. So I let him stay, giving him a dish of water and a few dead flies.

All summer long I kept his water fresh, killed flies for him and kept an eye out for his safety. Pickerel frogs sometimes live in caves, and I wondered if the dim light of the barn and the cool concrete floor made him think he had discovered a cave where the service was particularly good. That part of the barn serves as a passageway to my honey house, and I grew accustomed to seeing him as I went in and out of it. I came to regard him as a tutelary sprite, the guardian of the honey house, the Penate Melissus.

Then one day the health inspector came for his annual tour. Like Pharaoh, the health inspector is a fussy man. Once he gave me a hard time because there were a few stray honeybees in the honey house. Bees, he explained patiently, were insects, and regulations forbade insects in a food-processing plant. I pointed out, perhaps not so patiently, that these insects had made the food, and that until I took it from them, they were in continuous, complete and intimate contact with it. He gave up, but I know he didn't like it. So I wasn't sure how he'd react to the pickerel frog squatting outside the honey-house door with his bowl of water and mason-jar lid full of dead flies. But the health inspector is a brisk man, and he walked briskly by the frog and never saw him. I was thankful.

Years ago, in an introductory biology class, I cut up a frog, carefully laying aside the muscles, tracing the nerves and identifying the organs. I remember that as I discarded the carcass I was quite pleased with myself, for now I knew all about frogs and could go on to learn the remaining one or two things about which I still had some small ignorance. I was just about as smug as a gray tree frog on a white beehive.

In the years after that, and before I moved to the Ozarks, I also lived a brisk life, and although I never had much reason to doubt that I still knew all about frogs, I don't think I ever thought about them, for, like the health inspector, I never saw any.

Today my life has frogs aplenty and this delights me, but I am not so pleased with myself. My life hasn't turned out as I expected it would, for one thing. For another, I no longer know all about anything. I don't even know the first thing about frogs, for instance. There's nothing like having frogs fill up my windows or share my bed or require my protection to convince me of that.

I don't cut up frogs anymore, and I read more poetry than I did when I was twenty. I just read a couplet about the natural world by an anonymous Japanese poet. I copied it out and put it up on the wall above my desk today:

> *Unknown to me what resideth here*
> *Tears flow from a sense of unworthiness and gratitude.*

* * * * *

Anyone who has kept bees is a pushover for a swarm of them. We always drop whatever we are doing and go off to pick one up when asked to do so. It doesn't make sense, because from a standpoint of serious beekeeping and honey production a swarm isn't much good. Swarms are headed up by old queens with not much vitality or egg-laying potential left, and so a beekeeper should replace her with a new queen from a queen breeder. He will probably have to feed and coddle the swarm through its first year; it will seldom produce any extra honey the first season. And yet we always hive them.

There is something really odd about swarms, and I notice that beekeepers don't talk about it much, probably because it is the sort of thing we don't feel comfortable about trying to put into words, something the other side of rationality.

The second year I kept bees, I picked up my first swarm. I was in the middle of the spring beework, putting in ten to twelve hours a day, and very attuned to what the bees were doing out there in their hives. That day had begun with a heavy rainstorm, and so rather than working out in the beeyards, I was in the honey house making new equipment. By afternoon the rain had stopped, but the air was warm and heavy, charged and expectant. I began to feel odd, tense and anticipatory, and when the back of my neck began to prickle I decided to take a walk out to the new hives I had started. Near them, hanging pendulously from the branch of an apple tree, was a swarm of bees. Individual bees were still flying in from all directions, adding their numbers to those clinging around their queen.

In the springtime some colonies of bees, for reasons not well understood, obey an impulse to split in two and thus multiply by swarming. The worker bees thoughtfully raise a new queen bee for the parent colony, and then a portion of the bees gather with the old queen, gorge themselves with honey and fly out of the hive, never to return, leaving all memory of their old home behind. They cluster somewhere temporarily, such as on the branch of my apple tree. If a beekeeper doesn't hive them, scout bees fly from the cluster and investigate nearby holes and spaces, and report back to the cluster on the suitability of new quarters.

We know about two forms of honeybee communication. One is chemical: information about food sources and the wellbeing of the queen and colony is exchanged as bees continually feed one another with droplets of nectar which they have begun to process and chemically tag. The other form of communication is tactile: bees tell other bees about good things such as food or the location of a new home by patterned motions. These elaborate movements, which amount to a highly stylized map of landmarks, direction and the sun's position, are called the bee dance.

Different scout bees may find different locations for the swarm and return to dance about their finds. Eventually, sometimes after several days, an agreement is reached, rather like the arrival of the Sense of the Meeting among Quakers, and all the bees in the cluster fly off to their new home.

I watched the bees on my apple tree for a while with delight and pleasure, and then returned to the barn to gather up enough equipment to hive them. As I did so, I glanced up at the sky. It was still dark from the receding thunderstorm, but a perfect and dazzling rainbow arched shimmering against the deep blue sky, its curve making a stunning and pleasing contrast with the sharp inverted V of the barn roof. I returned to the apple tree and shook the bees into the new beehive, noticing that I was singing snatches of one of Handel's coronation anthems. It seemed as appropriate music to hive a swarm by as any I knew.

Since then, I have learned to pay attention in the springtime when the air feels electric and full of excitement. It was just so one day last week. I had been working quietly along the row of twelve hives in an outyard when the hair on the back of my neck began to stand on end. I looked up to see the air thick with bees flying in toward me from the north. The swarm was not from any of my hives, but for some reason bees often cluster near existing hives while they scout a new location. I closed up the hive I was working on and stood back to watch. I was near a slender post oak sapling, and the bees began to light on one of its lower limbs right next to my elbow. They came flying in, swirling as they descended, spiraling around me and the post oak until I was enveloped by the swarm, the air moving gently from the beat of their wings. I am not sure how long I stood there. I lost all sense of time and felt only elation, a kind of human emotional counterpart of the springlike, optimistic, burgeoning, state that the bees were in. I stood quietly; I was nothing more to the bees than an object to be encircled on their way to the spot where they had decided, in a way I could not know, to cluster. In another sense I was not remote from them at all, but was receiving all sorts of meaningful messages in the strongest way imaginable outside of human mental process and language. My skin was tingling as the bees brushed past and I felt almost a part of the swarm.

Eventually the bees settled down in the cluster. Regaining a more suitable sense of my human condition and responsibilities, I went over to my pickup and got the empty hive that I always carry with me during swarming season. I propped it up so that its entrance was just under the swarm. A frame of comb from another hive was inside and the bees in the cluster could smell it, so they began to walk up into the entrance. I watched, looking for the queen, for without her the swarm would die. It took perhaps twenty minutes for all of them to file in, and the queen, a long, elegant bee, was one of the last to enter.

I screened up the entrance and put the hive in the back of the pickup. After I was finished with my work with the other hives in the beeyard, I drove back home with my new swarm.

I should have ordered a new queen bee, killed the old one and replaced her, but in doing that I would have destroyed the identity of the swarm. Every colony of bees takes its essence, character and personality from the queen who is mother to all its members. As a commercial beekeeper, it was certainly my business to kill the old queen and replace her with a vigorous new one so that the colony would become a good honey producer.

But I did not.

In 1974, Hope Ryden, a filmmaker and photographer, proposed in a New York Times *article that the beaver be named New York's state animal. Six months later the state legislature agreed. Ryden's study of beavers is documented in* Lily Pond: Four Years with a Family of Beavers *(1989), a detailed account of the beavers' response to the environmental and seasonal changes in Lily Pond in Harriman State Park, New York. In this chapter from* Lily Pond, *Ryden confronts the dangers of the pond's thin ice and a snow storm to renew her acquaintance with the beavers when they emerge from their lodge for the first time that winter. Ryden has a knack for merging with the landscape and waiting patiently for new discoveries; here she describes a special moment when her patience was rewarded.*

From *Lily Pond: Four Years with a Family of Beavers*

ARCH CAME IN LIKE A LION, dropping three inches of wet snow on the park. Then, four days into the month, a cold wet drizzle coated the ground with a slippery glaze. Nevertheless, even though walking was hazardous, I was determined to visit the beaver house. But how to get there? I no longer trusted the pond ice to support my weight, nor could I make it to the lodge by land, for the dense laurel on the steep north bank was no more penetrable in winter than it had been in fall. In the end, I put my halogen lantern, my camera, my binoculars, and a few birch branches into my backpack, pulled on hip boots and then, hugging the shoreline, risked walking on the exceedingly thin and slippery ice.

The day was dark and a mist hung in the air. As I stepped onto the pond, I knew I would break through and my intuition proved correct. Twice I found myself knee deep in water. In the end, however, my effort was rewarded. For when I arrived at the lodge, I discovered a pool of water had opened beside it.

I tossed my token offering of birch branches on top of the weak ice that ringed this pool in the hope that a beaver would put in an appearance and climb out of the water to retrieve it. Thus I would have a rare opportunity to photograph the animal in a winter scene. Then I sat down on a wet rock beside the lodge and listened for beaver voices.

Ten weeks had passed since I had actually seen any member of my colony, and late-ly, since the colony had reverted to its same old nocturnal lifestyle, I had not heard much from them either. Had they wintered successfully? Had they stretched the two-week supply of food we brought them to last three months? Were all six beavers still alive inside the lodge?

While I sat quietly on a rock, wet snow began to fall. In such weather my camera is of little use, and so I packed it and my binoculars back into my bag and entertained myself by watching a pair of mallards waddle about on the ice. Migrant waterfowl were already returning. Then I waited in silence and allowed my mind to grow quiet. After a short while I heard a glug. A beaver had dived into the plunge hole that led into the pond and was about to make his debut in the open water directly in front of me.

The prospect of seeing one of my subjects again started my heart pounding, but I managed to hold still while I waited to discover who would surface. I was more than a little apprehensive that my presence so near to the lodge would alarm the animal. I need not have concerned myself over that possibility, however, for what surfaced was a mighty sleepy-looking creature. He floated about for a few seconds, then, after shaking his head like a dog, hauled himself onto a snow-crusted rock just six feet from where I sat. Who was this beaver? He looked too thin to be the Inspector General and too large to be either of the yearlings. And Lily I would recognize, fat or thin. Her soft gray muzzle and gentle questioning expression were characteristics that were uniquely hers.

The sleepy-looking beaver, draped on the rock, let his eyes close part way, and did not move at all. I, too, remained absolutely immobile for I don't know how long. Wet snowflakes, falling on my face and eyelashes, blurred my vision. Sooner or later I would have to raise my hand and wipe them away, a movement likely to startle the beaver. Better to alert him to my proximity with a quiet word or two in the hope he might hear something familiar and reassuring in my voice. And so I spoke.

"Don't be afraid," I said quietly. "You remember me."

And apparently he did, for after gazing at me for a few moments, he turned his sleepy attention from my wet face to his own, which he then proceeded to groom with his front paws. While I watched him wipe his cheeks and rub his ears, I failed to notice the appearance of another beaver. Silently, one of the kits had descended the plunge hole and come up for air beside the thin, dark adult. I kept right on talking.

"Well, hello there," I greeted him. "Glad to see you again, too."

The baby seemed as unperturbed by my presence as the adult. Both animals, in fact, appeared somewhat stupefied, as if dazed by the unaccustomed sensory load of light and odor and sound. Being icebound for three long months must have had a tranquilizing effect on them. As I continued to speak, they remained absolutely still.

Then, noiselessly, a second kit showed up and, as had the first, lined up beside the thin dark adult. I was delighted to know that both late-born youngsters had made it through winter despite the paucity of food in the family larder. And they looked to be in good health. The appearance of the second kit incited the first one to play, and in short order the two were rolling about in the water. I got the impression they were celebrating their new-found freedom and that they reveled in their own buoyancy and agility. And who wouldn't? Given another life, I might like to be a seal or otter or beaver—and for the same reason.

After a time, one of the kits swam over to me. By now he was fully alert and fixed his gaze directly on my face. Whatever he saw there apparently did not frighten him, for he quickly became distracted by the sight of the branches I had tossed onto the ice and went over to investigate them. He did not climb out of the water, however, as I had anticipated, but instead grasped the edge of the ice shelf with his front paws and pressed down on it, as if to break off a piece. When this did not work, he swam underneath the ice shelf until he was exactly below the spot where the branches rested. Then he rammed his head against it. After a couple of tries the ice shattered, and the little beaver popped up through broken shards and reached for a branch, which he then pulled underwater. A few moments later I heard gnawing sounds from inside the lodge.

So even baby beavers break ice! And how adept this youngster had been at it. Was the impulse to do so encoded in all beavers? Perhaps, but even so there was more to what I had seen than rote behavior, for there was nothing mindless about how the kit had approached the problem of getting the stick. Upon discovering it was beyond his grasp, he attempted at first to use his hands to dismantle the ice shelf upon which it rested. When this failed, he tried another tack. He swam underneath the icecap and punched it out from below.

No sooner had the little beaver brought evidence into the family's living quarters that birch branches were to be had, than the big, thin beaver, who meanwhile had returned to the lodge, emerged again. Like a navy icebreaker, he nosed his way into the floating shards and seized all the remaining branches. Clutching this twiggy bouquet in his teeth, he dived under the ice cover and vanished.

I fished my binoculars from my pack and scanned the shores for him. Falling snow made viewing difficult, but after a time I spotted him at my old station across the pond. He had swum eighty yards under the ice cap, emerged by way of an otter hole, and was peacefully eating his find where no kits could pester him for a share.

It was almost dark when I left, and as I made my way back along the south shore I once again broke through thin ice up to my knees. It was with a real sense of relief that I reached the dam. Upon climbing onto it, however, I saw that a band of water, nearly a foot wide, had opened alongside it during my brief absence. How had that happened?

As I walked the slippery crest, that gap of water made me nervous, and I had to steal a stick from the back side of the beavers' engineering work to give me support. With snow blowing in my eyes, I did not have much of a sense that winter was on its way out; yet a number of signs were pointing to that fact. Though the cold season was putting on a brave front, warm currents were at work under the ice, eroding it from below. Soon those two mallards I had watched earlier would be nesting in the saw grass.

I walked in four inches of snow a quarter mile down a closed park-road to where I had parked and rejoiced all the way. At least three members of my beaver colony had survived the killer season. And ice-out was near at hand.

ANNIE DILLARD
(1945–)

🌳

With the publication of Pilgrim at Tinker Creek, *which won the Pulitzer Prize for nonfiction in 1974, Annie Dillard established a style of nature writing that is now often imitated. Her essays about the Roanoke Valley of the Blue Ridge Mountains of West Virginia encompass the mystical as well as the humorous, and she "explores the neighborhood," in search of experience and a better understanding "about what it feels like to be alive." In these excerpts from* Pilgrim at Tinker Creek, *Dillard mixes narrative and natural history to examine the landscape of creek and meadow.*

Dillard's other work includes Tickets for a Prayer Wheel *(1974),* Teaching a Stone to Talk *(1982),* An American Childhood *(1987), and numerous essays.*

"Winter"

T SNOWED. It snowed all yesterday and never emptied the sky, although the clouds looked so low and heavy they might drop all at once with a thud. The light is diffuse and hueless, like the light on paper inside a pewter bowl. The snow looks light and the sky dark, but in fact the sky is lighter than the snow. Obviously the thing illuminated cannot be lighter than its illuminator. The classical demonstration of this point involves simply laying a mirror flat on the snow so that it reflects in its surface the sky, and comparing by sight this value to that of the snow. This is all very well, even conclusive, but the illusion persists. The dark is overhead and the light at my feet; I'm walking upside-down in the sky.

Yesterday I watched a curious nightfall. The cloud ceiling took on a warm tone, deepened, and departed as if drawn on a leash. I could no longer see the fat snow flying against the sky; I could see it only as it fell before dark objects. Any object at a distance—like the dead, ivy-covered walnut I see from the bay window—looked like a black-and-white frontispiece seen through the sheet of white tissue. It was like dying, this watching the world recede into deeper and deeper blues while the snow piled; silence swelled and extended, distance dissolved, and soon only concentration at the largest shadows let me make out the movement of falling snow, and that too failed. The snow on the yard was blue as ink, faintly luminous; the sky violet. The bay window betrayed me, and started giving me back the room's lamps. It was like dying, that growing dimmer and deeper and then going out.

Today I went out for a look around. The snow had stopped, and a couple of inches lay on the ground. I walked through the yard to the creek; everything was slate-blue and gunmetal and white, except for the hemlocks and cedars, which showed a brittle, secret green if I looked for it under the snow.

Lo and behold, here in the creek was a silly-looking coot. It looked like a black and gray duck, but its head was smaller; its clunky white bill sloped straight from the curve of its skull like a cone from its base. I had read somewhere that coots were shy. They were liable to take umbrage at a footfall, skitter terrified along the water, and take to the air. But I wanted a good look. So when the coot tipped tail and dove, I raced towards it across the snow and hid behind a cedar trunk. As it popped up again its neck was as rigid and eyes as blank as a rubber duck's in the bathtub. It paddled downstream, away from me. I waited until it submerged again, then made a break for the trunk of the Osage orange. But up it came all at once, as though the child in the tub had held the rubber duck under water with both hands, and suddenly released it. I froze stock-still, thinking that after all I really was, actually and at bottom, a tree, a dead tree perhaps, even a wobbly one, but a treeish creature nonetheless. The coot wouldn't notice that a tree hadn't grown in that spot the moment before; what did it know? It was new to the area, a mere dude. As tree I allowed myself only the luxury of keeping a wary eye on the coot's eye. Nothing; it didn't suspect a thing—unless, of course, it was just leading me on, beguiling me into scratching my nose, when the jig would be up once and for all, and I'd be left unmasked, untreed, with no itch and an empty creek. So.

At its next dive I made the Osage orange and looked around from its trunk while the coot fed from the pool behind the riffles. From there I ran downstream to the sycamore, getting treed in open ground again—and so forth for forty minutes, until it gradually began to light in my leafy brain that maybe the coot wasn't shy after all. That all this subterfuge was unnecessary, that the bird was singularly stupid, or at least not of an analytical turn of mind, and that in fact I'd been making a perfect idiot of myself all alone in the snow. So from behind the trunk of a black walnut, which was my present blind, I stepped boldly into the open. Nothing. The coot floated just across the creek from me, absolutely serene. Could it possibly be that I'd been flirting all afternoon with a *decoy?* No, decoys don't dive. I walked back to the sycamore, actually moving in plain sight not ten yards from the creature, which gave no sign of alarm or flight. I stopped; I raised my arm and waved. Nothing. In its beak hung a long, wet strand of some shore plant; it sucked it at length down its throat and dove again. I'll kill it. I'll hit the thing with a snowball, I really will; I'll make a mud-hen hash.

But I didn't even make a snowball. I wandered upstream, along smooth banks under trees. I had gotten, after all, a very good look at the coot. Now here were its tracks in the snow, three-toed and very close together. The wide, slow place in the creek by the road bridge was frozen over. From this bank at this spot in summer I can always see tadpoles, fat-bodied, scraping brown algae from a sort of shallow underwater ledge. Now I couldn't see the ledge under the ice. Most of the tadpoles were now frogs, and the frogs were buried alive in the mud at the bottom of the creek. They went to all that trouble to get out of the water and breathe air, only to hop back in before the first killing frost. The frogs of Tinker Creek are slathered in mud, mud at their eyes and mud at their nostrils; their damp skins absorb a muddy oxygen, and so they pass the dreaming winter.

Also from this bank at this spot in summer I can often see turtles by crouching low to catch the triangular poke of their heads out of water. Now snow smothered the ice; if it stays cold, I thought, and the neighborhood kids get busy with brooms, they can skate. Meanwhile, a turtle in the creek under the ice is getting oxygen by an almost incredible arrangement. It sucks water posteriorly into its large cloacal opening, where sensitive tissues filter the oxygen directly into the blood, as a gill does. Then the turtle discharges the water and gives another suck. The neighborhood kids can skate right over this curious rush of small waters.

Under the ice the bluegills and carp are still alive; this far south the ice never stays on the water long enough that fish metabolize all the oxygen and die. Farther north, fish sometimes die in this way and float up to the ice, which thickens around their bodies and holds them fast, open-eyed, until the thaw. Some worms are still burrowing in the silt, dragonfly larvae are active on the bottom, some algae carry on a dim photosynthesis, and that's about it. Everything else is dead, killed by the cold, or mutely alive in any of various still forms: egg, seed, pupa, spore. Water snakes are hibernating as dense balls, water striders hibernate as adults along the bank, and mourning cloak butterflies secret themselves in the bark of trees: all of these emerge groggily in winter thaws, to slink, skitter, and flit about in one afternoon's sunshine, and then at dusk to seek shelter, chill, fold, and forget.

The muskrats are out: they can feed under the ice, where the silver trail of bubbles that rises from their fur catches and freezes in streaming, glittering globes. What else? The birds, of course, are fine. Cold is no problem for warm-blooded animals, so long as they have food for fuel. Birds migrate for food, not for warmth as such. That is why, when so many people all over the country started feeding stations, southern birds like the mockingbird easily extended their ranges north. Some of our local birds go south, like the female robin; other birds, like the coot, consider *this* south. Mountain birds come down to the valley in a vertical migration; some of them, like the chickadees, eat not only seeds but such tiny fare as aphid eggs hid near winter buds and the ends of twigs. This afternoon I watched a chickadee swooping and dangling high in a tulip tree. It seemed astonishingly heated and congealed, as though a giant pair of hands had scooped a skyful of molecules and squeezed it like a snowball to produce this fireball, this feeding, flying, warm solid bit.

Other interesting things are going on wherever there is shelter. Slugs, of all creatures, hibernate, inside a waterproof sac. All the bumblebees and paper wasps are dead except the queens, who sleep a fat, numbed sleep, unless a mouse finds one and eats her alive. Honeybees have their own honey for fuel, so they can overwinter as adults, according to Edwin Way Teale, by buzzing together in a tightly packed, living sphere. Their shimmying activity heats the hive; they switch positions from time to time so that each bee gets its chance in the cozy middle and its turn on the cold outside. Ants hibernate en masse; the woolly bear hibernates alone in a bristling ball. Ladybugs hibernate under shelter in huge orange clusters sometimes the size of basketballs. Out West, people hunt for these overwintering masses in the mountains. They take them down to warehouses in the valleys, which pay handsomely. Then, according to Will Barker, the mail-order houses ship them to people who want them to eat garden aphids. They're mailed in the cool of night in boxes of old pine cones. It's a clever device: How do you pack a hundred living ladybugs? The insects naturally crawl deep into the depths of the pine cones; the sturdy "branches" of the opened cones protect them through all the bumpings of transit.

I crossed the bridge invigorated and came to a favorite spot. It is the spit of land enclosed in the oxbow of Tinker Creek. A few years ago I called these few acres the weed-field; they grew mostly sassafras, ivy, and poke. Now I call it the woods by the creek; young tulip grows there, and locust and oak. The snow on the wide path through the woods was unbroken. I stood in a little clearing beside the dry ditch that the creek cuts, bisecting the land, in high water. Here I ate a late lunch of ham sandwiches and wished I'd brought water and left more fat on the ham.

There was something new in the woods today—a bunch of sodden, hand-lettered signs tied to the trees all along the winding path. They said "SLOW," "Slippery When Wet," "Stop," "PIT ROW," "ESSO," and "BUMP!!" These signs indicated an awful lot of excitement over a little snow. When I saw the first one, "SLOW," I thought, sure, I'll go slow; I won't screech around on the unbroken path in the woods by the creek under snow. What was going on here? The other signs made it clear. Under "BUMP!!" lay, sure enough, a bump. I scraped away the smooth snow. Hand-fashioned of red clay, and now frozen, the bump was about six inches high and eighteen inches across. The slope, such as it was, was gentle; tread marks stitched the clay. On the way out I saw that I'd missed the key sign, which had fallen: "Welcome to the Martinsville Speedway." So my "woods by the creek" was a motorbike trail to the local boys, their "Martinsville Speedway." I had always wondered why they bothered to take a tractor-mower to these woods all summer long, keeping the many paths open; it was a great convenience to me.

Now the speedway was a stillnessway. Next to me in a sapling, a bird's nest cradled aloft a newborn burden of snow. From a crab apple tree hung a single frozen apple with blistered and shiny skin; it was heavy and hard as a stone. Everywhere through the trees I saw the creek run blue under the ledge of ice from the banks; it made a thin, metallic sound like foil beating foil.

When I left the woods I stepped into a yellow light. The sun behind a uniform layer of gray had the diffuse shine of a very much rubbed and burnished metal boss. On the mountains the wan light slanted over the snow and gouged out shallow depressions and intricacies in the mountains' sides I never knew were there. I walked home. No school today. The motorbike boys were nowhere in sight; they were probably skidding on sleds down the very steep hill and out onto the road. Here my neighbor's small children were rolling a snowman. The noon sun had dampened the snow; it caught in slabs, leaving green, irregular tracks on the yard. I just now discovered the most extraordinary essay, a treatise on making a snowman. ". . . By all means use what is ready to hand. In a fuel-oil burning area, for instance, it is inconceivable that fathers should sacrifice their days hunting downtown for lumps of coal for their children's snowmen's eyes. Charcoal briquettes from the barbecue are an unwieldy substitute, and fuel-oil itself is of course out of the question. Use pieces of rock, brick, or dark sticks; use bits of tire tread or even dark fallen leaves rolled tightly, cigarwise, and deeply inserted into sockets formed by a finger." Why, why in the blue-green world write this sort of thing? Funny written culture, I guess; we pass things on . . . .

* * * * *

"Nightwatch"

I stood in the Lucas Meadow in the middle of a barrage of grasshoppers. There must have been something about the rising heat, the falling night, the ripeness of grasses — something that mustered this army in the meadow where they have never been in such legions before. I must have seen a thousand grasshoppers, alarums and excursions clicking over the clover, knee-high to me.

I had stepped into the meadow to feel the heat and catch a glimpse of the sky, but these grasshoppers demanded my attention, and became an event in themselves. Every step I took detonated the grass. A blast of bodies like shrapnel exploded around me; the air burst and whirred. There were grasshoppers of all sizes, grasshoppers yellow, green and black, short-horned, long-horned, slant-faced, band-winged, spur-throated, cone-headed, pygmy, spotted, striped and barred. They sprang in salvos, dropped in the air, and clung unevenly to stems and blades with their legs spread for balance, as redwings ride cattail reeds. They clattered around my ears; they ricocheted off my calves with an instant clutch and release of tiny legs.

I was in shelter, but open to the sky. The meadow was clean, the world new, and I washed by my walk over the waters of the dam. A new, wild feeling descended upon me and caught me up. What if these grasshoppers were locusts, I thought; what if I were the first man in the world, and stood in a swarm?

I had been reading about locusts. Hordes of migrating locusts have always appeared in arid countries, and then disappeared as suddenly as they had come. You could actually watch them lay eggs all over a plain, and the next year there would be no locusts on the plain. Entomologists would label their specimens, study their structure, and never find a single one that was alive—until years later they would be overrun again. No one knew in what caves or clouds the locusts hid between plagues.

In 1921 a Russian naturalist named Uvarov solved the mystery. Locusts are grasshoppers: they are the same animal. Swarms of locusts are ordinary grasshoppers gone berserk.

If you take ordinary grasshoppers of any of several species from any of a number of the world's dry regions—including the Rocky Mountains—and rear them in glass jars under crowded conditions, they go into the migratory phase. That is, they turn into locusts. They literally and physically change from Jekyll to Hyde before your eyes. They will even change, all alone in their jars, if you stimulate them by a rapid succession of artificial touches. Imperceptibly at first, their wings and wing-covers elongate. Their drab color heightens, then saturates more and more, until it locks at the hysterical locust yellows and pinks. Stripes and dots appear on the wing-covers; these deepen to a glittering black. They lay more egg-pods than grasshoppers. They are restless, excitable, voracious. You now have jars full of plague.

Under ordinary conditions, inside the laboratory and out in the deserts, the eggs laid by these locusts produce ordinary solitary grasshoppers. Only under special conditions—such as droughts that herd them together in crowds near available food—do the grasshoppers change. They shun food and shelter and seek only the jostle and clack of their kind. Their ranks swell; the valleys teem. One fine day they take to the air.

In full flight their millions can blacken the sky for nine hours, and when they land, it's every man to your tents, O Israel. "A fire devoureth before them; and behind them a flame burneth: the land is as the garden of Eden before them, and behind them a desolate wilderness; yea, and nothing shall escape them." One writer says that if you feed one a blade of grass, "the eighteen components of its jaws go immediately into action, lubricated by a brown saliva which looks like motor oil." Multiply this action by millions, and you hear a new sound: "The noise their myriad jaws make when engaged in their work of destruction can be realized by any one who has fought a prairie fire or heard the flames passing along before a brisk wind, the low crackling and rasping." Every contour of the land, every twig, is inches deep in bodies, so the valleys seethe and the hills tremble. Locusts: it is an old story.

A man lay down to sleep in a horde of locusts, Will Barker says. Instantly the suffocating swarm fell on him and knit him in a clicking coat of mail. The metallic mouth parts meshed and pinched. His friends rushed in and woke him at once. But when he stood up, he was bleeding from the throat and wrists.

The world has locusts, and the world has grasshoppers. I was up to my knees in the world . . . .

🌳

*After she finished a film project in Wyoming in 1976, Gretel Ehrlich traded
her California city life for a ranching and writing life, where she "was able
to take up residence on earth with no alibis, no self-promoting schemes."
Her first book,* The Solace of Open Spaces *(1985), relates how the
Wyoming landscape becomes a source of comfort for her after the death of a
man she loved. In this essay, Ehrlich describes herding sheep by herself for
the first time; the experience teaches her how to find her way with little
guidance, in a place where "there's too much of everything."*

"From a Sheepherder's Notebook; Three Days"

WHEN THE PHONE RANG, it was John:
"Maurice just upped and quit and there ain't nobody else around, so you better get
packed. I'm taking you out to herd sheep." I walked to his trailerhouse. He smoked
impatiently while I gathered my belongings. "Do you know *anything* about herding
sheep after all this time?" he asked playfully. "No, not really." I was serious. "Well, it's
too late now. You'll just have to figure it out. And there ain't no phones up there either!"

He left me off on a ridge at five in the morning with a mare and a border collie.
"Last I saw the sheep, they was headed for them hills," he said, pointing up toward a
dry ruffle of badlands. "I'll pull your wagon up ahead about two miles. You'll see it. Just
go up that ridge, turn left at the pink rock, then keep agoing. And don't forget to bring
the damned sheep."

Morning. Sagesmell, sunsquint, birdsong, cool wind. I have no idea where I am,
how to get to the nearest paved road, or how to find the sheep. There are tracks going
everywhere so I follow what appear to be the most definite ones. The horse picks a path
through sagebrush. I watch the dog. We walk for several miles. Nothing. Then both sets
of ears prick up. The dog looks at me imploringly. The sheep are in the draw ahead.

Move them slow or fast? Which crossing at the river? Which pink rock? It's like
being a first-time mother, but mother now to two thousand sheep who give me the
kind of disdainful look a teenager would his parent and, with my back turned, can get
into as much trouble. I control the urge to keep them neatly arranged, bunched up by

the dog, and, instead, let them spread out and fill up. Grass being scarce on spring range, they scatter.

Up the valley, I encounter a slalom course of oil rigs and fenced spills I hadn't been warned about. The lambs, predictably mischievous, emerge dripping black. Freed from those obstacles, I ride ahead to find the wagon which, I admit, I'm afraid I'll never see, leaving the sheep on the good faith that they'll stay on their uphill drift toward me.

"Where are my boundaries?" I'd asked John.

"Boundaries?" He looked puzzled for a minute. "Hell, Gretel, it's all the outfit's land, thirty or forty miles in any direction. Take them anywhere they want to go."

On the next ridge I find my wagon. It's a traditional sheepherder's wagon, rounded top, tiny wood cookstove, bed across the back, built-in benches and drawers. The rubber wheels and long tongue make it portable. The camp tender pulls it (now with a pickup, earlier with teams) from camp to camp as the feed is consumed, every two weeks or so. Sheep begin appearing and graze toward me. I picket my horse. The dog runs for shade to lick his sore feet. The view from the dutch doors of the wagon is to the southeast, down the long slit of a valley. If I rode north, I'd be in Montana within the day, and next week I'll begin the fifty-mile trail east to the Big Horns.

Three days before summer solstice; except to cook and sleep I spend every waking hour outside. Tides of weather bring the days and take them away. Every night a bobcat visits, perched at a discreet distance on a rock, facing me. A full moon, helium-filled, cruises through clouds and is lost behind rimrock. No paper cutout, this moon, but ripe and splendid. Then Venus, then the North Star. Time for bed. Are the sheep bedded down? Should I ride back to check them?

Morning. Blue air comes ringed with coyotes. The ewes wake clearing their communal throats like old men. Lambs shake their flop-eared heads at leaves of grass, negotiating the blade. People have asked in the past, "What do you do out there? Don't you get bored?" The problem seems to be something else. There's too much of everything here. I can't pace myself to it.

Down the valley the sheep move in a frontline phalanx, then turn suddenly in a card-stacked sequential falling, as though they had turned themselves inside out, and resume feeding again in whimsical processions. I think of town, of John's trailerhouse, the clean-bitten lawn, his fanatical obsession with neatness and work, his small talk with hired hands, my eyesore stacks of books and notes covering an empty bed, John smoking in the dark of early morning, drinking coffee, waiting for daylight to stream in.

After eating I return to the sheep, full of queasy fears that they will have vanished and I'll be pulled off the range to face those firing-squad looks of John's as he says, "I knew you'd screw up. Just like you screw up everything." But the sheep are there. I can't stop looking at them. They're there, paralyzing the hillside with thousands of mincing feet, their bodies pressed together as they move, saucerlike, scanning the earth for a landing.

Thunderstorm. Sheep feed far up a ridge I don't want them to go over, so the dog, horse, and I hotfoot it to the top and ambush them, yelling and hooting them back down. Cleverly, the horse uses me as a windbreak when the front moves in. Lightning fades and blooms. As we descend quickly, my rein-holding arm looks to me like a blank stick. I feel numb. Numb in all this vividness. I don't seem to occupy my life fully.

Down in the valley again I send the dog "way around" to turn the sheep, but he takes the law into his own hands and chases a lamb off a cliff. She's wedged upside down in a draw on the other side of the creek. It will take twenty minutes to reach her, and the rest of the sheep have already trailed ahead. This numbness is a wrist twisting inside my throat. A lone pine tree whistles, its needles are novocaine. "In nature there are neither rewards nor punishments; there are only consequences." I can't remember who said that. I ride on.

One dead. Will she be reborn? And as what? The dog that nips lambs' heels into butchering chutes? I look back. The "dead" lamb convulses into action and scrambles up the ledge to find his mother.

Twin terrors: to be awake; to be asleep.

All day clouds hang over the Beartooth Mountains. Looking for a place out of the wind, I follow a dry streambed to a sheltered inlet. In front of me, there's something sticking straight up. It's the shell of a dead frog propped up against a rock with its legs crossed at the ankles. A cartoonist's idea of a frog relaxing, but this one's skin is paper-thin, mouth opened as if to scream. I lean close. "It's too late, you're already dead!"

Because I forgot to bring hand cream or a hat, sun targets in on me like frostbite. The dog, horse, and I move through sagebrush in unison, a fortress against wind. Sheep ticks ride my peeling skin. The dog pees, then baptizes himself at the water hole—full immersion—lapping at spitting rain. Afterward, he rolls in dust and reappears with sage twigs and rabbit brush strung up in his coat, as though in disguise—a Shakespearian dog. Above me, oil wells are ridge-top jewelry adorning the skyline with ludicrous sexual pumps. Hump, hump go the wells. Hump, hump go the drones who gather that black soup, insatiable.

We walk the fuselage of the valley. A rattlesnake passes going the other way; plenty of warning but so close to my feet I hop the rest of the day. I come upon the tin-bright litter of a former sheep camp: Spam cans flattened to the ground, their keys sticking up as if ready to open my grave.

Sun is in and out after the storm. In a long gully, the lambs gambol, charging in small brigades up one side, then the other. Ewes look on bored. When the lamb-fun peters out, the whole band comes apart in a generous spread the way sheep ranchers like them. Here and there lambs, almost as big as their mothers, kneel with a contagiously enthusiastic wiggle, bumping the bag with a goatlike butt to take a long draw of milk.

Night. Nighthawks whir. Meadowlarks throw their heads back in one ecstatic song after another. In the wagon I find a piece of broken mirror big enough to see my face: blood drizzles from cracked lips, gnats have eaten away at my ears.

To herd sheep is to discover a new human gear somewhere between second and reverse—a slow, steady trot of keenness with no speed. There is no flab in these days. But the constant movement of sheep from water hole to water hole, from camp to camp, becomes a form of longing. But for what?

The ten other herders who work for this ranch begin to trail their sheep toward summer range in the Big Horns. They're ahead of me, though I can't see them for the curve of the earth. One-armed Red, Grady, and Ed; Bob, who always bakes a pie when he sees me riding toward his camp; Fred, wearer of rags; "Amorous Albert"; Rudy, Bertha, and Ed; and, finally, Doug, who travels circuslike with a menagerie of goats, roosters, colts, and dogs and keeps warm in the winter by sleeping with one of the nannies. A peaceful army, of which I am the tail end, moving in ragtag unison across the prairie.

A day goes by. Every shiver of grass counts. The shallows and dapples in air that give grass life are like water. The bobcat returns nightly. During easy jags of sleep the dog's dream-paws chase coyotes. I ride to the sheep. Empty sky, an absolute blue. Empty heart. Sunburned face blotches brown. Another layer of skin to peel, to meet myself again in the mirror. A plane passes overhead—probably the government trapper. I'm waving hello, but he speeds away.

Now it's tomorrow. I can hear John's truck, the stock racks speak before I can actually see him, and it's a long time shortening the distance between us.

"Hello."

"Hello."

He turns away because something tender he doesn't want me to see registers in his face.

"I'm moving you up on the bench. Take the sheep right out the tail end of this valley, then take them to water. It's where the tree is. I'll set your wagon by that road."

"What road?" I ask timidly.

Then he does look at me. He's trying to suppress a smile but speaks impatiently.

"You can see to hell and back up there, Gretel."

I ride to the sheep, but the heat of the day has already come on sizzling. It's too late to get them moving; they shade up defiantly, their heads knitted together into a wool umbrella. From the ridge there's whooping and yelling and rocks being thrown. It's John trying to get the sheep moving again. In a dust blizzard we squeeze them up the road, over a sharp lip onto the bench.

Here, there's wide-open country. A view. Sheep string out excitedly. I can see a hundred miles in every direction. When I catch up with John I get off my horse. We stand facing each other, then embrace quickly. He holds me close, then pulls away briskly and scuffles the sandy dirt with his boot.

"I've got to get back to town. Need anything?"

"Naw . . . I'm fine. Maybe a hat . . ."

He turns and walks his long-legged walk across the benchland. In the distance, at the pickup, an empty beer can falls on the ground when he gets in. I can hear his radio as he bumps toward town. Dust rises like an evening gown behind his truck. It flies free for a moment, then returns, leisurely, to the habitual road—that bruised string which leads to and from my heart.

LESLIE MARMON SILKO
(1948–)

Leslie Marmon Silko, who is of Laguna Pueblo, Mexican, and Anglo descent, grew up in Laguna Pueblo in New Mexico. The traditional myth and ritual of her Indian ancestry provide the framework for her novels, stories, and poems. She has written the novels Almanac of the Dead *(1991) and* Ceremony *(1977) and the poetry and story collections* Laguna Woman *(1974) and* Storyteller *(1981). In the following essay, Silko explains the strong historical connection between clan and landscape and the Pueblo recognition of humans as part of the landscape, rather than separated from it.*

"Landscape, History, and the Pueblo Imagination"

FROM A HIGH ARID PLATEAU IN NEW MEXICO

YOU SEE THAT AFTER A THING IS DEAD, it dries up. It might take weeks or years, but eventually if you touch the thing, it crumbles under your fingers. It goes back to dust. The soul of the thing has long since departed. With the plants and wild game the soul may have already been borne back into bones and blood or thick green stalk and leaves. Nothing is wasted. What cannot be eaten by people or in some way used must then be left where other living creatures may benefit. What domestic animals or wild scavengers can't eat will be fed to the plants. The plants feed on the dust of these few remains.

The ancient Pueblo people buried the dead in vacant rooms or partially collapsed rooms adjacent to the main living quarters. Sand and clay used to construct the roof makes layers many inches deep once the roof has collapsed. The layers of sand and clay make for easy gravedigging. The vacant room fills with cast-off objects and debris. When a vacant room has filled deep enough, a shallow but adequate grave can be scooped in a far corner. Archaeologists have remarked over formal burials complete with elaborate funerary objects excavated in trash middens of abandoned rooms. But the rocks and adobe mortar of collapsed walls were valued by the ancient people. Because each rock had been carefully selected for size and shape, then chiseled to an even face. Even the pink clay adobe melting with each rainstorm had to be prayed over, then dug and carried some distance. Corn cobs and husks, the rinds and stalks and animal bones were not regarded by the ancient people as filth or garbage. The remains were merely resting at a mid-point in their journey back to dust. Human remains are not so different. They should rest with the bones and rinds where they all may benefit living creatures—small rodents and insects—until their return is completed. The remains of things—animals and plants, the clay and the stones—were treated with respect. Because for the ancient people all these things had spirit and being. The antelope merely consents to return home with the hunter. All phases of the hunt are conducted with love. The love the hunter and the people have for the Antelope People. And the love of the antelope who agree to give up their meat and blood so that human beings will not starve. Waste of meat or even the thoughtless handling of bones cooked bare will offend the antelope spirits. Next year the hunters will vainly search the dry plains for antelope. Thus it is necessary to return carefully the bones and hair, and the stalks and leaves to the earth who first created them. The spirits remain close by. They do not leave us.

The dead become dust, and in this becoming they are once more joined with the Mother. The ancient Pueblo people called the earth the Mother Creator of all things in this world. Her sister, the Corn Mother, occasionally merges with her because all succulent green life rises out of the depths of the earth.

Rocks and clay are part of the Mother. They emerge in various forms, but at some time before, they were smaller particles or great boulders. At a later time they may again become what they once were. Dust.

A rock shares this fate with us and with animals and plants as well. A rock has being or spirit, although we may not understand it. The spirit may differ from the spirit we know in animals or plants or in ourselves. In the end we all originate from the depths of the earth. Perhaps this is how all beings share in the spirit of the Creator. We do not know.

FROM THE EMERGENCE PLACE

Pueblo potters, the creators of petroglyphs and oral narratives, never conceived of removing themselves from the earth and sky. So long as the human consciousness remains *within* the hills, canyons, cliffs, and the plants, clouds, and sky, the term *landscape,* as it has entered the English language, is misleading. "A portion of territory the eye can comprehend in a single view" does not correctly describe the relationship between the human being and his or her surroundings. This assumes the viewer is somehow *outside* or *separate from* the territory he or she surveys. Viewers are as much a part of the landscape as the boulders they stand on. There is no high mesa edge or mountain peak where one can stand and not immediately be part of all that surrounds. Human identity is linked with all the elements of Creation through the clan: you might belong to the Sun Clan or the Lizard Clan or the Corn Clan or the Clay Clan.[1] Standing deep within the natural world, the ancient Pueblo understood the thing as it was—the squash blossom, grasshopper, or rabbit itself could never be created by the human hand. Ancient Pueblos took the modest view that the thing itself (the landscape) could not be improved upon. The ancients did not presume to tamper with what had already been created. Thus *realism,* as we now recognize it in painting and sculpture, did not catch the imaginations of Pueblo people until recently.

The squash blossom itself is *one thing:* itself. So the ancient Pueblo potter abstracted what she saw to be the key elements of the squash blossom—the four symmetrical petals, with four symmetrical stamens in the center. These key elements, while suggesting the squash flower, also link it with the four cardinal directions. By representing only its intrinsic form, the squash flower is released from a limited meaning or restricted identity. Even in the most sophisticated abstract form, a squash flower or a cloud or a lightning bolt became intricately connected with a complex system of relationships which the ancient Pueblo people maintained with each other, and with the populous natural world they lived within. A bolt of lightning is itself, but at the same time it may mean much more. It may be a messenger of good fortune when summer rains are needed. It may deliver death, perhaps the result of manipulations by the Gunnadeyahs, destructive necromancers. Lightning may strike down an evil-doer. Or lightning may strike a person of good will. If the person survives, lightning endows him or her with heightened power.

Pictographs and petroglyphs of constellations or elk or antelope draw their magic in part from the process wherein the focus of all prayer and concentration is upon the thing itself, which, in its turn, guides the hunter's hand. Connection with the spirit dimensions requires a figure or form which is all-inclusive. A "lifelike" rendering of an elk is too restrictive. Only the elk *is* itself. A *realistic* rendering of an elk would be only one particular elk anyway. The purpose of the hunt rituals and magic is to make contact with *all* the spirits of the Elk.

The land, the sky, and all that is within them—the landscape—includes human beings. Interrelationships in the Pueblo landscape are complex and fragile. The unpredictability of the weather, the aridity and harshness of much of the terrain in the high plateau country explain in large part the relentless attention the ancient Pueblo people gave the sky and the earth around them. Survival depended upon harmony and cooper-

[1]Clan—*A social unit composed of families sharing common ancestors who trace their lineage back to the Emergence where their ancestors allied themselves with certain plants or animals or elements.* [Silko's note]

ation not only among human beings, but among all things—the animate and the less animate, since rocks and mountains were known to move, to travel occasionally.

The ancient Pueblos believed the Earth and the Sky were sisters (or sister and brother in the post-Christian version). As long as good family relations are maintained, then the Sky will continue to bless her sister, The Earth, with rain, and the Earth's children will continue to survive. But the old stories recall incidents in which troublesome spirits or beings threaten the earth. In one story, a malicious ka'tsina, called the Gambler, seizes the Shiwana, or Rainclouds, the Sun's beloved children.[2] The Shiwana are snared in magical power late one afternoon on a high mountain top. The Gambler takes the Rainclouds to his mountain stronghold where he locks them in the north room of his house. What was his idea? The Shiwana were beyond value. They brought life to all things on earth. The Gambler wanted a big stake to wager in his games of chance. But such greed, even on the part of only one being, had the effect of threatening the survival of all life on earth. Sun Youth, aided by old Grandmother Spider, outsmarts the Gambler and the rigged game, and the Rainclouds are set free. The drought ends, and once more life thrives on earth.

THROUGH THE STORIES WE HEAR WHO WE ARE

All summer the people watch the west horizon, scanning the sky from south to north for rain clouds. Corn must have moisture at the time the tassels form. Otherwise pollination will be incomplete, and the ears will be stunted and shriveled. An inadequate harvest may bring disaster. Stories told at Hopi, Zuñi, and at Acoma and Laguna describe drought and starvation as recently as 1900. Precipitation in west-central New Mexico averages fourteen inches annually. The western pueblos are located at altitudes over 5,600 feet above sea level, where winter temperatures at night fall below freezing. Yet evidence of their presence in the high desert plateau country goes back ten thousand years. The ancient Pueblo people not only survived in this environment, but many years they thrived. In A.D. 1100 the people at Chaco Canyon had built cities with apartment buildings of stone five stories high. Their sophistication as sky-watchers was surpassed only by Mayan and Inca astronomers. Yet this vast complex of knowledge and belief, amassed for thousands of years, was never recorded in writing.

Instead, the ancient Pueblo people depended upon collective memory through successive generations to maintain and transmit an entire culture, a world view complete with proven strategies for survival. The oral narrative, or "story," became the medium in which the complex of Pueblo knowledge and belief was maintained. Whatever the event

---

[2]Ka'tsina–*Ka'tsinas are spirit beings who roam the earth and who inhabit kachina masks worn in Pueblo ceremonial dances.* [Silko's note]

or the subject, the ancient people perceived the world and themselves within that world as part of an ancient continuous story composed of innumerable bundles of other stories.

The ancient Pueblo vision of the world was inclusive. The impulse was to leave nothing out. Pueblo oral tradition necessarily embraced all levels of human experience. Otherwise, the collective knowledge and beliefs comprising ancient Pueblo culture would have been incomplete. Thus stories about the Creation and Emergence of human beings and animals into this World continue to be retold each year for four days and four nights during the winter solstice. The "humma-hah" stories related events from the time long ago when human beings were still able to communicate with animals and other living things. But, beyond these two preceding categories, the Pueblo oral tradition knew no boundaries. Accounts of the appearance of the first Europeans in Pueblo country or of the tragic encounters between Pueblo people and Apache raiders were no more and no less important that stories about the biggest mule deer ever taken or adulterous couples surprised in cornfields and chicken coops. Whatever happened, the ancient people instinctively sorted events and details into a loose narrative structure. Everything became a story.

Traditionally everyone, from the youngest child to the oldest person, was expected to listen and to be able to recall or tell a portion, if only a small detail, from a narrative account or story. Thus the remembering and retelling were a communal process. Even if a key figure, an elder who knew much more than others, were to die unexpectedly, the system would remain intact. Through the efforts of a great many people, the community was able to piece together valuable accounts and crucial information that might otherwise have died with an individual.

Communal storytelling was a self-correcting process in which listeners were encouraged to speak up if they noted an important fact or detail omitted. The people were happy to listen to two or three different versions of the same event or the same humma-hah story. Even conflicting versions of an incident were welcomed for the entertainment they provided. Defenders of each version might joke and tease one another, but seldom were there any direct confrontations. Implicit in the Pueblo oral tradition was the awareness that loyalties, grudges, and kinship must always influence the narrator's choices as she emphasizes to listeners this is the way *she* has always heard the story told. The ancient Pueblo people sought a communal truth, not an absolute. For them this truth lived somewhere within the web of differing versions, disputes over minor points, outright contradictions tangling with old feuds and village rivalries.

A dinner-table conversation, recalling a deer hunt forty years ago when the largest mule deer ever was taken, inevitably stimulates similar memories in listeners. But hunting stories were not merely after-dinner entertainment. These accounts contained information of critical importance about behavior and migration patterns of mule deer. Hunting stories carefully described key landmarks and locations of fresh water. Thus a deer-hunt story might also serve as a "map." Lost travelers, and lost piñon-nut gathers, have been saved by sighting a rock formation they recognize only because they once heard a hunting story describing this rock formation.

The importance of cliff formations and water holes does not end with hunting stories. As offspring of the Mother Earth, the ancient Pueblo people could not conceive of themselves within a specific landscape. Location, or "place," nearly always plays a central role in the Pueblo oral narratives. Indeed, stories are most frequently recalled as people are passing by a specific geographical feature or the exact place where a story takes place. The precise date of the incident often is less important than the place or location of the happening. "Long, long ago," "a long time ago," "not too long ago," and "recently" are usually how stories are classified in terms of time. But the places where the stories occur are precisely located, and prominent geographical details recalled, even if the landscape is well-known to listeners. Often because the turning point in the narrative involved a peculiarity or special quality of a rock or tree or plant found only at that place. Thus, in the case of many of the Pueblo narratives, it is impossible to determine which came first: the incident or the geographical feature which begs to be brought alive in a story that features some unusual aspect of this location.

There is a giant sandstone boulder about a mile north of Old Laguna, on the road to Paguate. It is ten feet tall and twenty feet in circumference. When I was a child, and we would pass this boulder driving to Paguate village, someone usually made reference to the story about Kochininako, Yellow Woman, and the Estrucuyo, a monstrous giant who nearly ate her. The Twin Hero Brothers saved Kochininako, who had been out hunting rabbits to take home to feed her mother and sisters. The Hero Brothers had heard her cries just in time. The Estrucuyo had cornered her in a cave too small to fit its monstrous head. Kochininako had already thrown to the Estrucuyo all her rabbits, as well as her moccasins and most of her clothing. Still the creature had not been satisfied. After killing the Estrucuyo with their bows and arrows, the Twin Hero Brothers slit open the Estrucuyo and cut out its heart. They threw the heart as far as they could. The monster's heart landed there, beside the old trail to Paguate village, where the sandstone boulder rests now.

It may be argued that the existence of the boulder precipitated the creation of a story to explain it. But sandstone boulders and sandstone formations of strange shapes abound in the Laguna Pueblo area. Yet most of them do not have stories. Often the crucial element in a narrative is the terrain—some specific detail of the setting.

A high dark mesa rises dramatically from a grassy plain fifteen miles southeast of

Laguna, in an area known as Swanee. On the grassy plain one hundred and forty years ago, my great-grandmother's uncle and his brother-in-law were grazing their herd of sheep. Because visibility on the plain extends for over twenty miles, it wasn't until the two sheepherders came near the high dark mesa that the Apaches were able to stalk them. Using the mesa to obscure their approach, the raiders swept around from both ends of the mesa. My great-grandmother's relatives were killed, and the herd lost. The high dark mesa played a critical role: the mesa had compromised the safety which the openness of the plains had seemed to assure. Pueblo and Apache alike relied upon the terrain, the very earth herself, to give them protection and aid. Human activities or needs were maneuvered to fit the existing surroundings and conditions. I imagine the last afternoon of my distant ancestors as warm and sunny for late September. They might have been traveling slowly, bringing the sheep closer to Laguna in preparation for the approach of colder weather. The grass was tall and only beginning to change from green to a yellow which matched the late-afternoon sun shining off it. There might have been comfort in the warmth and the sight of the sheep fattening on good pasture which lulled my ancestors into their fatal inattention. They might have had a rifle whereas the Apaches had only bows and arrows. But there would have been four or five Apache raiders, and the surprise attack would have canceled any advantage the rifles gave them.

Survival in any landscape comes down to making the best use of all available resources. On that particular September afternoon, the raiders made better use of the Swanee terrain than my poor ancestors did. Thus the high dark mesa and the story of the two lost Laguna herders became inextricably linked. The memory of them and their story resides in part with the high black mesa. For as long as the mesa stands, people within the family and clan will be reminded of the story of that afternoon long ago. Thus the continuity and accuracy of the oral narratives are reinforced by the landscape—and the Pueblo interpretation of that landscape is *maintained.*

THE MIGRATION STORY: AN INTERIOR JOURNEY

The Laguna Pueblo migration stories refer to specific places—mesas, springs, or cottonwood trees—not only locations which can be visited still, but also locations which lie directly on the state highway route linking Paguate village with Laguna village. In travelling this road as a child with older Laguna people I first heard a few of the stories from that much larger body of stories linked with the Emergence and Migration.[3] It

---

[3]The Emergence–*All the human beings, animals, and life which had been created emerged from the four worlds below when the earth became habitable.*

The Migration–*The Pueblo people emerged into the Fifth World, but they had already been warned they would have to travel and search before they found the place they were meant to live.* [Silko's note]

may be coincidental that Laguna people continue to follow the same route which, according to the Migration story, the ancestors followed south from the Emergence Place. It may be that the route is merely the shortest and best route for car, horse, or foot traffic between Laguna and Paguate villages. But if the stories about boulders, springs, and hills are actually remnants from a ritual that retraces the creation and emergence of the Laguna Pueblo people as a culture, as the people they became, then continued use of that route creates a unique relationship between the ritual-mythic world and the actual, everyday world. A journey from Paguate to Laguna down the long incline of Paguate Hill retraces the original journey from the Emergence Place, which is located slightly north of the Paguate village. Thus the landscape between Paguate and Laguna takes on a deeper significance: the landscape resonates the spiritual or mythic dimension of the Pueblo world even today.

Although each Pueblo culture designates a specific Emergence Place—usually a small natural spring edged with mossy sandstone and full of cattails and wild watercress—it is clear that they do not agree on any single location or natural spring as the one and only true Emergence Place. Each Pueblo group recounts its own stories about Creation, Emergence, and Migration, although they all believe that all human beings, with all the animals and plants, emerged at the same place and at the same time.[4]

Natural springs are crucial sources of water for all life in the high desert plateau country. So the small spring near Paguate village is literally the source and continuance of life for the people in the area. The spring also functions on a spiritual level, recalling the original Emergence Place and linking the people and the spring water to all other people and to that moment when the Pueblo people became aware of themselves as they are even now. The Emergence was an emergence into a precise cultural identity. Thus the Pueblo stories about the Emergence and Migration are not to be taken as literally as the anthropologists might wish. Prominent geographical features and landmarks which are mentioned in the narratives exist for ritual purposes, not because the Laguna people actually journeyed south for hundreds of years from Chaco Canyon or Mesa Verde, as the archaeologists say, or eight miles from the site of the natural springs at Paguate to the sandstone hilltop at Laguna.

The eight miles, marked with boulders, mesas, springs, and river crossings, are actually a ritual circuit or path which marks the interior journey the Laguna people made: a journey of awareness and imagination in which they emerged from being within the earth and from everything included in earth to the culture and people they became, dif-

---

[4]Creation–*Tse'itsi'nako, Thought Woman, the Spider, thought about it, and everything she thought came into being. First she thought of three sisters for herself, and they helped her think of the rest of the Universe, including the Fifth World and the four worlds below. The Fifth World is the world we are living in today. There are four previous worlds below this world.* [Silko's note]

ferentiating themselves for the first time from all that had surrounded them, always aware that interior distances cannot be reckoned in physical miles or in calendar years.

The narratives linked with prominent features of the landscape between Paguate and Laguna delineate the complexities of the relationship which human beings must maintain with the surrounding natural world if they hope to survive in this place. Thus the journey was an interior process of the imagination, a growing awareness that being human is somehow different from all other life—animal, plant, and inanimate. Yet we are all from the same source: the awareness never deteriorated into Cartesian duality, cutting off the human from the natural world.

The people found the opening into the Fifth World too small to allow them or any of the animals to escape. They had sent a fly out through the small hole to tell them if it was the world which the Mother Creator had promised. It was, but there was the problem of getting out. The antelope tried to butt the opening to enlarge it, but the antelope enlarged it only a little. It was necessary for the badger with her long claws to assist the antelope, and at last the opening was enlarged enough so that all the people and animals were able to emerge up into the Fifth World. The human beings could not have emerged without the aid of antelope and badger. The human beings depended upon the aid and charity of the animals. Only through interdependence could the human beings survive. Families belonged to clans, and it was by clan that the human being joined with the animal and plant world. Life on the high arid plateau became viable when the human beings were able to imagine themselves as sisters and brothers to the badger, antelope, clay, yucca, and sun. Not until they could find a viable relationship to the terrain, the landscape they found themselves in, could they *emerge*. Only at the moment the requisite balance between human and *other* was realized could the Pueblo people become a culture, a distinct group whose population and survival remained stable despite the vicissitudes of climate and terrain.

Landscape thus has similarities with dreams. Both have the power to seize terrifying feelings and deep instincts and translate them into images—visual, aural, tactile—into the concrete where human beings may more readily confront and channel the terrifying instincts or powerful emotions into rituals and narratives which reassure the individual while reaffirming cherished values of the group. The identity of the individual as a part of the group and the greater Whole is strengthened, and the terror of facing the world alone is extinguished.

Even now, the people at Laguna Pueblo spend the greater portion of social occasions recounting recent incidents or events which have occurred in the Laguna area. Nearly always, the discussion will precipitate the retelling of older stories about similar incidents or other stories connected with a specific place. The stories often contain disturbing or provocative material, but are nonetheless told in the presence of children and women. The effect of these inter-family or inter-clan exchanges is the reassurance for each person that she or he will never be separated or apart from the clan, no matter what might happen. Neither the worst blunders or disasters nor the greatest financial prosperity and joy will ever be permitted to isolate anyone from the rest of the group. In the ancient times, cohesiveness was all that stood between extinction and survival, and, while the individual certainly was recognized, it was always as an individual simultaneously bonded to family and clan by a complex bundle of custom and ritual. You are never the first to suffer a grave loss or profound humiliation. You are never the first, and you understand that you will probably not be the last to commit or be victimized by a repugnant act. Your family and clan are able to go on at length about others now passed on, others older or more experienced than you who suffered similar losses.

The wide deep arroyo near the Kings Bar (located across the reservation borderline) has over the years claimed many vehicles. A few years ago, when a Viet Nam veteran's new red Volkswagon rolled backwards into the arroyo while he was inside buying a six-pack of beer, the story of his loss joined the lively and large collection of stories already connected with that big arroyo. I do not know whether the Viet Nam veteran was consoled when he was told the stories about the other cars claimed by the ravenous arroyo. All his savings of combat pay had gone for the red Volkswagon. But this man could not have felt any worse than the man who, some years before, had left his children and mother-in-law in his station wagon with the engine running. When he came out of the liquor store his station wagon was gone. He found it and its passengers upside down in the big arroyo. Broken bones, cuts and bruises, and a total wreck of the car. The big arroyo has a wide mouth. Its existence needs no explanation. People in the area regard the arroyo much as they might regard a living being, which has a certain character and personality. I seldom drive past that wide deep arroyo without feeling a familiarity with and even a strange affection for this arroyo. Because as treacherous as it may be, the arroyo maintains a strong connection between human beings and the earth. The arroyo demands from us the caution and attention that constitute respect. It is this sort of respect the old believers have in mind when they tell us we must respect and love the earth.

Hopi Pueblo elders have said that the austere and, to some eyes, barren plains and hills surrounding their mesa-top villages actually help to nurture the spirituality of the Hopi *way.* The Hopi elders say the Hopi people might have settled in locations far more lush where daily life would not have been so grueling. But there on the high silent sandstone mesas that overlook the sandy arid expanses stretching to all horizons, the Hopi elders say the Hopi people must "live by their prayers" if they are to survive. The Hopi way cherishes the intangible: the riches realized from interaction and interrelationships with all beings above all else. Great abundances of material things, even food, the Hopi elders believe, tend to lure human attention away from what is most valuable and important. The views of the Hopi elders are not much different from those elders in all the Pueblos.

The bare vastness of the Hopi landscape emphasizes the visual impact of every plant, every rock, every arroyo. Nothing is overlooked or taken for granted. Each ant, each lizard, each lark is imbued with great value simply because the creature is there, simply because the creature is alive in a place where any life at all is precious. Stand on the mesa edge at Walpai and look west over the bare distances toward the pale blue outlines of the San Francisco peaks where the ka'tsina spirits reside. So little lies between you and the sky. So little lies between you and the earth. One look and you know that simply to survive is a great triumph, that every possible resource is needed, every possible ally—even the most humble insect or reptile. You realize you will be speaking with all of them if you intend to last out the year. Thus it is that the Hopi elders are grateful to the landscape for aiding them in their quest as spiritual people.

DIANA KAPPEL-SMITH
(1951–)

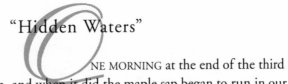

*Diana Kappel-Smith explores the winter world of a northern Vermont hill
farm in her first book,* Wintering *(1979). Mixing scientific and artistic perspectives, she writes of the natural world she finds in the snow-covered landscape and weaves together her personal thoughts and experiences, along with
events of farm life. She engages our imagination through her curiosity; and,
although there are not always answers to her questions, she provides plenty of
imaginative ideas about what might be happening in the natural world. In
this essay, she delves into the mysteries of sugar maple trees and the frenzied
human reaction at the first sign of a maple sap run during a spring thaw.*

"Hidden Waters"

ONE MORNING at the end of the third
week in March it began to rain, and when it did the maple sap began to run in our
woods. As I drove along the hill road to home, there was a mist rising everywhere as if
the ground were the bowl of a volcano; serrated ranks of spruce and fir rose through the
streaming vapor like jagged teeth, rooted in ridges that curved like the jawbones of
gigantic animals. I felt suddenly as if I would, any minute, be swallowed up by this
thawing landscape, gulped in with no more eulogy that a steamy burp issuing between
two ranks of champing spruce. Everything in and under the snow was suddenly awash,
and as suddenly exposed to the sharp frosts that were still coming: what were the seeds,
roots, meadow voles, doing now?

It rained for most of the afternoon and the mountains were sealed away behind a
curtain that was the color of wet plastic. In the woods the sap tanks were filling steadily;
next morning we would boil in our first syrup of the season. During the middle of the
afternoon I put on my yellow coveralls and armed myself with shears and a pole-saw
and went out to prune my apple trees, my rite of March; clipping dead twigs, disentan-
gling conflicting limbs, and lopping skyward tendencies. I am a small woman and I
can't pick apples too high in the air.

All afternoon I was aware of what was going on down in the sugar woods, and even
involved as I was with decisions among the apple twigs, I kept my eye on the two small
maples behind the house. They didn't seem to be doing anything at all; a hoax. If I were

a maple in the spring rain, I would be swollen with juice, red in the face, my heartbeat tripled; I would be howling and dancing, threshing my arms against the sky! But trees are introverts. Everything that goes on there goes on *inside* until they are ready for their final statement of faith, for which we have to wait another month or two. Then they will let loose their flowers, a mist of sexually loaded parachutes dangling from little silks; and finally their leaves. Trees are like anything else—if one doesn't need to know anything about their insides, one can go on thinking that they don't have any. Ignorance can be bliss.

The Indians of the eastern woods were the first people to make maple sugar. It isn't difficult to see how they got the idea; in the first thaws every broken maple twig end and every porcupine-chewed patch of bark bleeds sap. Some of this sap dribbles down the trunk of the tree and is distilled by the sun into golden sugar drops; in March and April I have harvested these candies myself, picking them from the bark with heavy competition from a pair of overcharged, newly wakened chipmunks. The Indians—Pennacooks, Laurentians, Mahicans, Malecites—had their spring groves all over the Northeast and into Canada: they slashed the tree bark with tomahawks and boiled their sugar by dropping hot stones into birchbark troughs and hollowed tree trunks full of sap. It was a laborious way to boil anything, but the only way to boil in flammable pots. Then as now it took about thirty-two gallons of sap to make eight pounds of sugar. With the river ice going and the snow melting fast the men were off fishing, after fat hare, the first geese; and sugaring was women's work. It is still a common thing here for women to do the boiling, to keep all the float-valves set just so on the big steel evaporating rigs, and to keep the filters rinsed, and the hot syrup graded and canned.

I don't make my syrup alone. I've gone into partnership now with a friend. He cuts the wood and keeps the fire going and I help with the boiling where I can, and I make myself useful by climbing up on the woodpile and throwing down wood. In the evening I like to go out and sit on the stump of a beech tree that I cut many winters ago, to watch the towering geyser of sparks which explodes from the top of the smokestack when he shakes the fire. Sometimes I make fresh doughnuts to dip in hot cups of syrup, and I make coffee from boiling sap so that the brew has the gritty taste of the woods still in it.

I am always awed and stirred by these trees, perhaps because they seem so unmoved even in the midst of their most violent season. We don't collect our sap in pails; we collect it the modern way by more or less letting it collect itself. The sap flows downhill from the tapholes through a plumbing system made of plastic tubing. The tubes are hitched together with clamps and widgets like a giant set of Tinkertoys. The tubes run into small black pipes and the small pipes run into bigger pipes. A final two-inch pipe lets the whole thirty acres' worth of maples run into the holding tanks, from which the evaporator draws its slow supply. In the days when we hung pails in the woods a good run was signaled by the muffled plinks of dripping sap, which was a gentle enough sound, though the trees could still fill their attendant pails twice in one day if they felt like it. The pipeline system is more brutal. I have seen our two-inch pipe gushing sap as though it were a firehose. I have watched the holding tanks filling up at a brisk 300 gallons an hour. And all the while the trees stand; the trees stand on their slope, mute and unbudged. What—I have wondered this more than once in March and April, when my life is run according to the maples' fickle moods—what is *going on?*

In my last year at college I took an elective course at the Proctor Maple Research Lab. The work done there with maple trees is a kind of grassroots project, sponsored by the university and staffed by inspired people who do their science with their boots on. One year there they cut an entire maple, which weighed several tons, and hoisted the top part over the stump and monitored both the branch and root systems for months, only to discover that, no, the sap does not come up from the roots in the spring. Old Wives' Tale No. 1 debunked: what then? They discovered that some trees have sweeter sap than others by a factor of many hundred percent. They stuck hypodermics into baby maples and discovered that sweet trees are sweet from birth; that productivity varies in maples as it does in cows, in direct proportion to the quality of their parentage and the quality of their feed—a maple's feed being plentiful sunlight and dry sloped ground. They put sap-drip measurers and pressure cuffs and thermometers in and on their trees, and had a roomful of dials and recording needles to monitor the condition of their patients. They made detailed charts. They made maple syrup. They boiled syrup with oil, gas, and woodchips. They boiled syrup in experimental evaporators which looked like the rear ends of moonrockets. After a few years some patterns began to emerge from all of this, a body of knowledge which like all such bodies raised more questions that it answered.

For sap to run at all there has to be a thaw, with no wind to chill the twigs. For the sap to run well it has to have been below freezing for at least forty-eight hours before the thaw began. The sap run is a live process; if the thin films and spokes of living tissue in the tree are killed, no sap runs at all. The fact that such a tiny rise in temperature can bring about such a huge response means that there must be some live "trigger" involved anyhow; an enzyme that kicks suddenly into play, completes its work, retires. What enzyme? What work? No one is sure.

The sap runs from the tapholes because the tree pushes it out; this is the unexpected thing. During a thaw the whole tree expands under the pressure of its sap. The tree in winter is a closed hydraulic system and during a sap run it can build internal pressures of up to twenty-four pounds per square inch. After a while—even if it stays warm, or instantly if the temperature should drop below freezing again—the pressures reverse and become negative. Given the chance then, the trees might reabsorb all of the sap that they pushed out hours before.

If the weather is right the sap will run from the trees any time for six weeks or so after the leaves have fallen—sometime in November—until the new leaves arrive. During winter warm spells the tree are grudging with their sap as if they were half asleep. After mid-March here the trees are at their touchiest and most responsive; if the weather cooperates then the trees *push*. What we wait for is classic sugaring weather—a span of icy nights and soft, clear, windless days. But weather can surprise everyone. It is as though the winter, being as strong as it is, omniscient, the ruler here, has entered a pitched battle with the forces that would have it go, go; and the trees and ourselves are caught in the crossfire.

In the first spring that I sugared here we had a monster run; there was a sleeting blizzard which lasted for three days, it was 33° F, and the trees were plastered with slush as though they were wearing bulky gray socks. The sap gushed, steadily, all that time. We boiled around the clock for three days and the sap tanks overflowed just the same. Two friends and I took turns firing, boiling, and dozing off. When we fed the fire we had to wear an extra pair of wool pants to protect our thighs from the heat, and asbestos gloves layered with silver duct-tape, and we had a seven-foot-long section of aluminum pipe to shake the fire down. Even protected as we were, we had scorch marks along our arms where our shirt cuffs had fallen open, and around our wrists where the gloves had slipped. By the third day we all felt as though we were locked in a losing war with the fires of the underworld. We took turns walking the three-quarters of a mile up to the barn to feed the sheep. I remember going down into the woods again through the timeless dusk of that blizzard, coming back to the sugarhouse, which was rumbling and steaming, its smokestack shooting columns of sparks that flew up like stars, and thinking that this was a forge built for dwarves. We looked like dwarves; swarthy and thick. What were the dwarves doing? Refining gold . . . ? Of course. Yes.

A run like that happens only two or three times in the career of any one sugarmaker, which is just as well. No one can predict it, though; so lay in a spare store of firewood, buy extra syrup drums; no one knows how the trees work. But we do know that after every run the bark of the trees has gained in water content and the wood has lost, and the frost resistance that was built up so carefully in the fall has been gently eroded; all the water columns in the sapwood have to be set in place again, ready for the leaves.

Toward the end of April the sap runs get scanty again as though the maples were moving on to other things. The syrup that we make then is dark and more and more heavily flavored, and finally it begins to smell and taste bad. The chemistry of the tree has suddenly changed; from one hour to the next we smell the change. The last rank syrup is shipped away for curing tobacco, and we pull our taps and wash the tubing and the tanks and the evaporator, and call it a year. There are spring beauties blooming then on the high ground under the trees, but the trees don't look any different than they did before. Except that if one looks closely at their buds one can see pale curves where the bud-scales once overlapped, and have, just, pulled apart.

TERRY TEMPEST WILLIAMS
(1955–)

Between 1983 and 1986, Great Salt Lake rose to an unprecedented height of over four thousand feet, destroying wetland areas of northern Utah and the home of many species of birds. Meanwhile, Terry Tempest Williams's mother was dying of ovarian cancer. In Refuge: An Unnatural History of Family and Place *(1991), the author, a naturalist-in-residence at Utah Museum of Natural History in Salt Lake City, tells the story of family and natural disaster, establishing a strong link between her Mormon heritage and the Utah desert. This personal style of nature writing enhances our understanding of the spiritual connection between humans and the natural world. She describes this best through her own identification with the birds and isolated terrain of the Utah desert, where she learns "how to find grace among spiders with a poisonous bite."*

"Long-Billed Curlews"

I FOUND THE LONG-BILLED CURLEWS at Curlew Valley. A dozen hovered over me like banshees,

"Cur-lee! Cur-lee! Cur-lee!"

I was in their territory and they did not like it. Because of their camouflage, those in the grasses were difficult to see. Movement was my only clue. I counted seven adults. Most were pecking and probing the overgrazed landscape, plucking out multitudes of grasshoppers in between the stubble. Others were contesting the boundaries of competing curlews as they chased each other with heads low in a running crouch. Two curlews faced each other, with necks extended, their long bills pointing toward the sky. They looked ready to fence. Tense gestures, until one bird backed down and flew. The triumphant curlew stepped forward and fluttered its strong, pointed wings above its head. Cinnamon under-feathers flashed like the bright slip of a Spanish dancer.

Female curlews, slightly larger than the males, were prostrate, their necks stretched outward from their bodies. I suspected they were on nests and did not disturb them.

Burr buttercups grew between the grasses like snares, and in prairie dogs' abandoned holes black widows, the size of succulent grapes, reigned.

The hostility of this landscape teaches me how to be quiet and unobtrusive, how to find grace among spiders with a poisonous bite. I sat on a lone boulder in the midst of the curlews. By now, they had grown accustomed to me. This too, I found encouraging—that in the face of stressful intrusions, we can eventually settle in. One begins to almost trust the intruder as a presence that demands greater intent toward life.

On a day like today when the air is dry and smells of salt, I have found my open space, my solitude, and sky. And I have found the birds who require it.

There is something unnerving about my solitary travels around the northern stretches of Great Salt Lake. I am never entirely at ease because I am aware of its will. Its mood can change in minutes. The heat alone reflecting off the salt is enough to drive me mad, but it is the glare that immobilizes me. Without sunglasses, I am blinded. My eyes quickly burn on Salt Well Flats. It occurs to me that I will return home with my green irises bleached white. If I return at all.

The understanding that I could die on the salt flats is no great epiphany. I could die anywhere. It's just that in the foresaken corners of Great Salt Lake there is no illusion of being safe. You stand in the throbbing silence of the Great Basin, exposed and alone. On these occasions, I keep tight reins on my imagination. The pearl-handed pistol I carry in my car lends me no protection. Only the land's mercy and a calm mind can save my soul. And it is here I find grace.

It's strange how deserts turn us into believers. I believe in walking in a landscape of mirages, because you learn humility. I believe in living in a land of little water because life is drawn together. And I believe in the gathering of bones as a testament to spirits that have moved on.

If the desert is holy, it is because it is a forgotten place that allows us to remember the sacred. Perhaps that is why every pilgrimage to the desert is a pilgrimage to the self. There is no place to hide, and so we are found.

In the severity of a salt desert, I am brought down to my knees by its beauty. My imagination is fired. My heart opens and my skin burns in the passion of these moments. I will have no other gods before me.

Wilderness courts our souls. When I sat in church throughout my growing years, I listened to teachings about Christ in the wilderness for forty days and forty nights, reclaiming his strength, where he was able to say to Satan, "Get thee hence." When I imagined Joseph Smith kneeling in a grove of trees as he received his vision to create a new religion, I believed their sojourns into nature were sacred. Are ours any less?

There is a Mormon scripture, from the Doctrine and Covenants section 88:44-47, that I carry with me:

The earth rolls upon her wings, and the sun giveth
his light by day, and the moon giveth her light
by night, and the stars also give their light, as
they roll upon their wings in their glory, in the
midst of the power of God.
Unto what shall I liken these kingdoms that ye may
understand?
Behold all these are kingdoms and any man who
hath seen any or the least of these hath seen God
moving in his majesty and power.

I pray to the birds.

I pray to the birds because I believe they will carry the messages of my heart upward. I pray to them because I believe in their existence, the way their songs begin and end each day—the invocations and benedictions of Earth. I pray to the birds because they remind me of what I love rather than what I fear. And at the end of my prayers, they teach me how to listen.

Hundreds of white pelicans appear—white against blue. They turn, disappear. Reappear, black against blue. They turn, disappear. Reappear, white against blue. Through my binoculars, I can see their bright orange bills, many with the characteristic knobs associated with courtship.

The grassy banks of Teal Spring are a welcome reprieve from the barren country I have come from. This is just one of the many small ponds at Locomotive Springs, ten miles from Curlew Valley. It is classified by the Utah Division of Wildlife Resources as a "first-magnitude marsh," which means a place with a stable water supply used by waterfowl for nesting, migration, and wintering. I would call it a first-magnitude marsh simply because it's green.

Brooke will come later this evening. Until then, I shall curl up in the grasses like a bedded animal and dream.

Marsh music. Red-wing blackbirds. Yellow-headed blackbirds. Song sparrows. Barn swallows snapping mosquitoes on the wing. Herons traversing the sky.

Brooke arrives and we walk.

The sign TEAL SPRING is silhouetted against a numinous sky. Its reflection in the pond looks like a black cross. We listen to the catcall of a redhead. Thousands of birds seem to be speaking behind us. We turn around and find only a fortress of greasewood.

Settling into our sleeping bag, I nestle into Brooke's body. We are safe. With our arms around each other, we watch ibis after ibis, heron after heron, teal after teal, fly over us. A few stars appear. We try counting them, until finally the sweet whimperings of shorebirds seduce us into sleep.

Sunrise. Teal Spring is transformed. The pinks and lavenders of the night before have been exchanged for the vitality of yellows and blues. Even the rushes, whose black reflection bled into the water twelve hours earlier, are golden. Instead of the stalks predominating, morning light has struck their flowering heads like a match. Small flames flicker on each tip.

To spend a night at the marsh is to wax and wane with birdsong. At sunset and for an hour or so afterward, the pitch and frenzy of birds is so high, so frantic, idle conversation is impossible. But after midnight, silence. The depth and stillness of Great Salt Lake comes over the wetlands like a mother's calming hand. Morning approaches slowly, until each voice in the marsh awakens.

Brooke and I walk miles across the northwestern wetlands and alkaline flats of the lake. Salt crystals attached to the mud look like blistered skin. The sun is searing and the black gnats are almost intolerable. Relief comes only through concentration, losing ourselves in the studied behavior of birds.

Marbled godwits forage the flats with avocets and stilts. It would be easy to confuse the godwits with curlews, except for their bicolored bills that point upward, not down. And I find their character very different from curlews—more trusting, more gentle, more calm. When a curlew is near, the air is stirred; they are anxious and aggressive. Godwits are serene. They demand little from you except the patience to observe. Curlews cause guilt. You are reminded of your intrusion, that you do not belong.

As we walked along an eroding dike, flush with the roaring lake, a blue heron flies off its nest leaving four large eggs. The nest is built of dried greasewood on an old weathered fence that fans out like an accordion. Two ravens hover with eyes on the eggs. We leave quickly, so the heron can return.

Walking back toward Teal Spring, we discover a dead curlew. Its body lies fixed, encrusted with salt. We kneel down and run our fingers down its long, curved bill. Brooke ponders over the genetic information a species is born with, the sophistication of cells and the memory held inside a gene pool. It is the embryology of a curlew that informs the stubby, straight beak of a chick to take a graceful curve down.

I say a silent prayer for the curlew, remembering the bond of two days before when I sat in their valley nurtured by solitude. I ask the curlew for cinnamon-barred feathers and take them.

They do not come easily.

FURTHER READING

Austin, Mary. *The Land of Little Rain.* Boston: Houghton Mifflin Co., 1903; Albuquerque: Univ. of New Mexico Press, 1974.

———*The Flock.* Boston: Houghton Mifflin, 1906.

———*Lost Borders.* New York: Harper & Bros., 1909.

———*The Lands of the Sun.* Boston: Houghton Mifflin, 1927.

———*The Land of Journeys' Ending.* New York: Century, 1924; Tucson: University of Arizona Press, 1983.

———*Earth Horizon.* Boston: Houghton Mifflin, 1932.

Bird, Isabella. *A Lady's Life in the Rocky Mountains.* New York: Putnam's, 1879-80; Norman: Univ. of Oklahoma Press, 1960.

Carson, Rachel. *Under the Sea-Wind: A Naturalist's Picture of Ocean Life.* New York: Oxford University Press, 1941, 1952.

———*The Sea Around Us.* New York: Oxford University Press, 1950; Simon & Schuster, 1958; rev. ed., Oxford Univ. Press, 1961.

———*The Edge of the Sea.* Boston: Houghton Mifflin, 1955.

———*Silent Spring.* Boston: Houghton Mifflin, 1962.

———*The Sense of Wonder.* New York: Harper & Row, 1965, 1987.

Cooper, Susan Fenimore. *Rural Hours.* New York: G.P. Putnam, 1850; rev. ed., Boston: Houghton Mifflin, 1887; Syracuse: Syracuse Univ. Press, 1968.

Dillard, Annie. *Pilgrim at Tinker Creek.* New York: Harper & Row, 1974.

———*Teaching a Stone to Talk: Expeditions and Encounters.* New York: Harper & Row, 1982.

Ehrlich, Gretel. *The Solace of Open Spaces.* New York: Viking 1985.

———*Islands, the Universe, Home.* New York: Viking, 1991.

Hoover, Helen. *The Long-Shadowed Forest.* New York: Norton, 1963.

———*The Gift of the Deer.* New York: Knopf, 1966

———*A Place in the Woods.* New York: Knopf, 1969.

———*The Years of the Forest.* New York: Knopf, 1973.

Hubbell, Sue. *A Country Year: Living the Questions.* New York: Random House, 1986.

———*A Book of Bees.* New York: Random House, 1988.

Kappel-Smith, Diana. *Wintering.* Boston: Little, Brown & Co., 1979.

———*Night Life.* Boston: Little, Brown & Co., 1990.

Kumin, Maxine. *In Deep: Country Essays.* New York: Viking, 1987.

———*Up Country: Poems of New England.* New York: Harper & Row, 1972.

———*Nurture.* New York: Viking, 1989.

Lamb, May Wynne. *Life in Alaska: The Reminiscenses of a Kansas Woman, 1916–1919.* Ed. Dorothy Wynne Zimmerman. Lincoln: Univ. of Nebraska Press, 1988.

Le Guin, Ursula K. *Buffalo Gals and Other Animal Presences.* Santa Barbara: Capra Press, 1987.

———*Always Coming Home.* New York: Harper & Row, 1985.

———"A Very Warm Mountain." *Parabola.* Vol. 5, no.4., Fall 1980.

Leister, Mary. *Wildlings.* Owing Mills, Maryland: Stemmer House Publishers, 1976.

———*Seasons at Heron Pond: Wildlings of Air, Earth and Water.* Owings Mills, MD: Stemmer House, 1981.

Rawlings, Marjorie Kinnan. *The Yearling.* New York: Charles Scribner's Sons, 1938.

———*Cross Creek.* New York: Charles Scribner's Sons, 1942.

Ryden, Hope. *America's Last Wild Horses.* New York: Dutton, 1970.

———*God's Dog: A Celebration of the North American Coyote.* New York: Viking, 1979.

———*Lily Pond.* New York: William Morrow & Co., Inc., 1989.

———*Bobcat Year.* New York: Nick Lyons Books, 1990.

Silko, Leslie Marmon. *Ceremony.* New York: Viking, 1977.

———"Landscape, History, and the Pueblo Imagination." *Antaeus.* No. 57, Autumn 1986.

———*Almanac of the Dead.* New York: Simon & Schuster, 1991.

Thaxter, Celia Laighton. *Among the Isles of Shoals.* New York: James R. Osgood & Co., 1873; Boston: Houghton Mifflin, 1892.

———*An Island Garden.* Boston: Houghton Mifflin, 1894, 1988.

Williams, Terry Tempest. *Pieces of White Shell: A Journey to Navajoland.* New York: Scribner's, 1984.

———*Refuge: An Unnatural History of Family and Place.* New York: Random House, 1991.

Wright, Mabel Osgood. *The Friendship of Nature: A New England Chronicle of Birds and Flowers.* New York: Macmillan, 1894.

Zwinger, Ann Haymond. *Beyond the Aspen Grove.* New York: Random House, 1970, 1981.

———*Run, River, Run.* New York: Harper & Row, 1975.

———*Wind in the Rock.* New York: Harper & Row, 1978.

———*A Desert Country Near the Sea: A Natural History of the Cape Region of Baja California.* New York: Harper & Row, 1983.

——— *The Mysterious Lands.* New York: E.P. Dutton, 1989.

PERMISSIONS

Excerpts from *A Lady's Life in the Rocky Mountains,* by Isabella L. Bird. New Edition copyright © 1960 by the University of Oklahoma Press.

"The Marginal World" from *The Edge of the Sea,* by Rachel Carson. Copyright © 1955 by Rachel L. Carson. Copyright © renewed 1983 by Roger Christie. Reprinted by permission of Houghton Mifflin Company. All rights reserved.

Excerpts from *Rural Hours* by Susan Fenimore Cooper with an introduction by David Jones, copyright © 1968. Reprinted by permission of Syracuse University Press.

Excerpts from *Pilgrim at Tinker Creek* by Annie Dillard. Copyright © 1974 by Annie Dillard. Reprinted by permission of HarperCollins Publishers.

"From a Sheepherder's Notebook: Three Days" from *The Solace of Open Spaces* by Gretel Ehrlich. Copyright © 1985 by Gretel Ehrlich. Used by permission of Viking Penguin, a division of Penguin Books USA Inc.

"King Weather" is reprinted from *The Long-Shadowed Forest* by Helen Hoover, by permission of W.W. Norton & Company, Inc. Copyright © 1963 by Helen Hoover and Adrian Hoover. Copyright renewed 1991.

"Spring" reprinted from *A Country Year: Living the Questions* by Sue Hubbell. Copyright © 1983, 1984, 1985, 1986 by Sue Hubbell. Reprinted by permission of Random House, Inc.

"Hidden Waters" from *Wintering* by Diana Kappel-Smith. Copyright © 1979, 1980, 1982, 1983, 1984 by Diana Kappel-Smith. By permission of Little, Brown and Company.

"Journal—Late Winter–Spring 1978," from *In Deep—Country Essays* by Maxine Kumin. Copyright © 1987 by Maxine Kumin. Used by permission of Viking Penguin, a division of Penguin Books USA Inc.

"The Kuskokwim River" by May Wynne Lamb is reprinted from *Life in Alasaka: The Reminiscences of a Kansas Woman, 1916–1919,* edited by Dorothy Wynne Zimmerman, by permission of University of Nebraska Press. Copyright © 1988, University of Nebraska Press.

"A Very Warm Mountain" by Ursula K. Le Guin. Copyright © 1980 by Ursula K. Le Guin; first appeared in *Parabola;* reprinted by permission of the author and the author's agent, Virginia Kidd.